Children in the Crossfire

Patricia Marlett

Scriptures from the King James Bible
Published in the United States of America
Published by High Tower Publishing

First Edition - 2017   ISBN: 978-0-9994680-2-9
Second Edition - 2022   ISBN: 978-0-9994680-2-9

High Tower Publications
2 Samuel 22:3

Acknowledgement

I will always, and forevermore, acknowledge and give thanks to God. I honor, praise and give the glory to my heavenly Father; for it is by His grace, that I am blessed. He is my inspiration and with the gift He has bestowed upon me, I write in His honor to glorify His name.

Also, deep appreciation to my husband, Mark, for his unwavering love, support, and dedication he gives as I pursue my passion. You are my rock, I love you.

Dedication

This book is dedicated to all who seek
the Kingdom of Heaven.

Table of Content

Note from the Author

If any man speak, let him speak as the oracles
of God; if any man minister, let him do it as
of the ability which God giveth: that God
in all things may be glorified through Jesus
Christ, to whom be praise and dominion for
ever and ever. Amen.
1 Peter 4:11

I t is with honor and glory to our heavenly Father that I take great pleasure in presenting this book to share the truth of God's Word as taught in the Scriptures, and to assure each person who reads the content on the following pages that everything God created and provided is for you.

It has always been about you when God established the foundation of all His creation as we read in the Bible and continues throughout eternity. I hope you gain insight of how much you are truly loved, and how desirous the Father is for you to be with Him today and forever.

God made all things possible through His Son, Jesus, when He gave man a new and better covenant. As a beneficiary of this testament, one of the many gifts is the free will to personally decide if we want a life with Him, one that is eternal. Though it is by our choice, God wants all His children to come home to the Kingdom of Heaven

We can be with our Father this very moment, spiritually, if we become one in spirit with His Son, Jesus. The first step is a desire to have a relationship with God and become a born-again child of the Father. In Christ, we are changed from a sinner to a saint and secured as a joint-heir through Jesus in the Kingdom.

I pray you are inspired to seek God and accept His Word as the guidepost for your life and maintain a relationship with your heavenly Father. Not simply know of Him, but fall in love with Him, learn His nature and understand what He has done for you, and what He expects of you, His child.

As a child to the parent, we should want our Father's love and a close bond with Him more than anything, ever. Only God can heal a broken body whether it is physical or emotional, only God can supply for personal and professional prosperity, and only God can give us eternal life. There is absolutely nothing permanent on this planet as this earthen place will one day be made anew to receive the New Jerusalem which will be the eternal home of every believer.

God's love, mercy, and grace are forever present and will always protect and provide for His children. We are His most precious creation, made in His likeness, for His pleasure, never forgotten or forsaken. Promises, blessings, gifts, and power are within His Kingdom, and we are personally responsible to acquire the knowledge that God has set forth in His Word, so that we may partake of these Kingdom treasures.

It is vital to understand the role of Christ and His purpose in fulfilling the Father's plan and to accept the Holy Spirit as our tutor who teaches all things of God and is our advocate in the Kingdom. This is crucial to living in the spirit and receiving all that He has prepared for you.

There will appear a redundancy within this book, for when speaking of God, the Son, and the Holy Spirit, all are God; and yet, He presents Himself as separate personages for man's purpose. Also in mentioning the Kingdom of Heaven and the Kingdom of Earth is to clarify there are two distinct kingdoms to consider when speaking of the battleground between God and Lucifer. A conscious effort has been made to keep the repetitiveness to a minimum.

With forethought, there are Scriptures appropriately placed to serve as a reference to what God's Word says as the focus is on His truth. Also, some Scriptures may be used more than once for an appropriate application of God's Word to the subject matter.

Our relationship with our heavenly Father is defined in our belief, trust, and unwavering faith. We are not lost souls wandering aimlessly and helpless throughout this life, but saints made righteous and holy in Christ for the Father.

Introduction

And all thy children shall be taught of the Lord; and great shall be the peace of thy children.
Isaiah 54:13

As you read each section within this book, try to envision a scene of how it must have been in the Kingdom of Heaven and later in the Kingdom of Earth. The two kingdoms represent the backdrop, or stage with the lead characters in the Kingdom of Heaven as God, the Word, the Holy Ghost, and Lucifer. The scene opens in the Kingdom of Heaven, but quickly progresses to the Kingdom of Earth where all the action takes place. In the Kingdom of Earth, it begins with Adam (man) and his wife, Eve, and Lucifer (Satan) with the introduction of Christ.

Throughout the performances of the main characters are many others who play a significant role such as Noah, Abraham, Sarah, Moses, Job, David, Solomon, Joseph, Mary, and so forth. Notice that initially with the lead characters in the Kingdom of Heaven that Christ and Satan aren't mentioned because the Word becomes Christ, and Lucifer's name changes to Satan once in the Kingdom of Earth. All the people,

Jews and Gentiles, are the *extras* required on a set possibly with some action on their part, but typically without dialogue.

In most stories, there is an antagonist; good versus evil, so even here in the Kingdom of Heaven where it all begins, we can garner who the antagonist is, Lucifer. From the onset of man's existence, we have been predisposed to our nature. Man has not created a thought or emotion that has not first existed within the Kingdom of Heaven. There is no novelty to man, and yet, we pride ourselves on our worldly acquired wisdom. It's foolishness on our part and sets the stage for Lucifer to engage and trap us in self-righteousness. Where do you think self-righteousness came from?

Today, our novels and movies are themed from the origin of what transpired between God and Lucifer. Meaning, the conflict we witness in many storylines from cowboys to villains in space. Yes, it goes back that far to the beginning of God's creation.

I hope you find it an interesting tale, but more pertinent, an interesting truth of two kings and two kingdoms as war is waged and the winner triumphs, for good always prevails. However, keep in mind this is not a battle that catches God off-guard, for He created all, including Lucifer.

Along with a free will, angels had the ability to process thoughts and express emotions, for these are required to use a free will. How else could Lucifer oppose his Almighty King?

For nearly six-thousand years, the battle continues to be waged on Earth, and we the people are the targeted subject. We are children caught in the crossfire between good and evil, life and death; between two kings with one provision to determine our fate, a free will. It is all about you, for you are now on center stage and a decision is imminent. Which king will you serve?

An Overview

But seek ye first the kingdom of God,
and his righteousness; and all these
things shall be added unto you.
Matthew 6:33

We are all children of God, even unbelievers, born from the seed of the first Adam, the man formed by the hand of God. In preparation for the second Adam, Christ, from the generations after Abraham, the father of all nations, a covenant was established by God with Abraham which gives each person the ability to receive Christ, for He was born from the lineage of David. He is our only way to the Kingdom of Heaven, to the Father, for an eternal life with our Almighty King.

This book is meant to bring the believer, and the unbeliever, to a crossroad where for a moment you push the pause button on your life to seriously evaluate if you are truly living according to the riches of God's Word. And if an unbeliever, to strongly consider the consequences of your decision because in the end what awaits is either eternal life, or the finality of death.

The decisions every person makes, knowingly or unbeknownst, affects their life each and every day and that of their loved ones. In short, it's a matter of living a life blessed by God, or cursed by Satan depending on which god's principles you are following. God gives His children blessings, while Satan places curses upon your life and keeps you in bondage.

It is uncomfortable for many to talk about Satan in the present tense; however, for the remaining duration of time before Christ returns, this is his Kingdom and you are born into it to deal with his persuasions. His objective is to keep you from God.

God has a plan for man's life when He created Adam. However, it didn't begin with Adam as you may have thought, but rather with Lucifer in the Kingdom of Heaven. Lucifer's defiance and war against his Creator set the precedence for the initial deception and example of self-righteousness and unbelief. His actions were a sin against the Almighty King. Here is where sin began, not in the Garden of Eden but in the Kingdom of Heaven.

In God's sovereignty and the Creator of all, it isn't just a matter of God knowing what will occur, but that He set forth in His Almighty plan the redemption of man. God is omnipresent and omnipotent; the Alpha and the Omega, the same yesterday, today, tomorrow, and forever; never changing.

God, Himself, has a plan of His own for the sole purpose of wanting His Kingdom filled with children; however, God didn't want robots but children who would want Him for their Father. It is the most beautiful love story ever told from the author of love, for God is love.

1

Rebellion in the Kingdom

Man's history began not in the Garden of Eden but in the Kingdom of Heaven. It didn't start with the first Adam but with second Adam, Jesus. The second Adam was before the first Adam, for Christ was the Word manifesting all of God's creation. As God spoke, the Word brought everything into existence. The Kingdom of Heaven existed before the Kingdom of Earth and before there was man there were angels.

Deception occurred in the Kingdom of Heaven before Adam in the Garden of Eden. Lucifer's defying act to overthrow the governing powers of the Almighty King was the origination of sin with the spinoff of self-righteousness and unbelief. All the afflictions that came upon Adam happened because of and through Lucifer.

Typically, we think our story of man begins in the Garden, but in actuality it goes further back into the Kingdom of Heaven. Lucifer set the precedence for Adam's deception, and thus, spirit death.

God created both angels and man with a free will, and it's easy to be swayed to believe in anything that seems reasonable. We witness this when one-third of the angels within the Kingdom chose to stand along-side Lucifer, believing he would oust the Creator.

Today, Lucifer is still seeking to build an army of people, along with his fallen angels, to oppose the Almighty King of all Creation. To build his fortress requires not just unbelievers, but to gain believers to his camp. His plan to keep everyone from God.

It delights him to deceive the Christians away from God, for his objective has not changed in nearly six-thousand years. In fact, there will be a final attempt to claim the temple in Jerusalem, sit on the throne and call himself God. It will be a climactic culmination of all his efforts before he is defeated for all time by the Son of God.

The high-ranking archangels have names, positions, and responsibilities. As we see everything of God's Kingdom is in a trinity, so also is the number of the prominent angels. They are Michael, Gabriel, and Lucifer. Something to take notice of is the position each holds. For example, Michael is a warrior angel, Gabriel a messenger angel, and Lucifer a worship angel. God had already set forth the commanding high-ranking angels with responsibilities required for a future event; a time when a messenger angel and a warrior angel would be needed in the Kingdom of Earth. There is order within God's Kingdom.

Lucifer was one of the high-ranking archangels with the charge of directing the angels in worship of the Almighty King; one whose ministry surrounded the heart of Heaven dwelling eternally in the very presence of God. *Son of man, take up a lamentation upon the king of Tyrus, and say unto him, Thus saith the Lord God; Thou sealest up the sum, full of wisdom, and perfect in beauty. Thou hast been in Eden the garden of God; every precious stone was thy covering, the sardius, topaz, and the diamond, the beryl, the onyx, and the jasper, the sapphire, the emerald, and the carbuncle, and gold: the workmanship of thy tabrets and of thy pipes was prepared in thee in the day that thou wast created. Thou art the anointed cherub that covereth; and I have set thee so: thou wast upon the holy mountain of God; thou hast walked up and down in the midst of the stones of fire. Thou wast perfect in thy ways from the day that thou wast created, till iniquity was found in thee.* Ezekiel 28:12-15 We have validation for Lucifer's position in the Kingdom of Heaven and his presence before the Almighty King.

God declared him perfectly made. However, because of Lucifer's exceeding beauty, greatness, and knowledge of the Kingdom, he became pompous and prideful believing he should hold the position as the Almighty King of the Kingdom of Heaven.

Because of his rebellious attempt to overthrow the throne of God along with one-third of the angels who chose to follow him, all were expelled to Earth. *How art thou fallen from heaven, O Lucifer, son of the morning! how art thou cut down to the ground, which didst weaken the nations! For thou hast said in thine heart, I will ascend into heaven, I will exalt my throne above the stars of God: I will sit also upon the mount of the congregation, in the sides of the north: I will ascend above the heights of the clouds; I will be like the most High. Yet thou shalt be brought down to hell, to the sides of the pit.* Isaiah 14:12-15 Lucifer was familiar with the Kingdom of Earth and the Garden of Eden before his fall: *Thou hast been in Eden the garden of God.*

When Lucifer was removed from the Kingdom of Heaven, the only place of his decent that he could have *fallen* to was the Kingdom of Earth; therefore, Lucifer was in residence before Adam. As an archangel, Lucifer had the ability to travel back and forth between these two kingdoms, Heaven and Earth, at will. In Heaven his name was Lucifer, *son of the morning*; however, when sent to Earth, his name changed to Satan, *adversary* or *accuser*.

God created man from the very soil of the Earth, formed him into clay and breathed into his nostrils the breath of life and named him Adam which means *earth*, or in Hebrew, *adamah*. He made man with a body, soul, and spirit and placed His most precious creation, fashioned in His likeness and image, in the Kingdom of Earth in a special garden eastward of Eden called the *Garden of Eden*. God made him king of the Kingdom of Earth, ruler over all the inhabitants including naming the animals that would occupy the land.

When Adam and Eve lived in the Garden of Eden, Lucifer, now referred to as Satan, was familiar with the layout of the Garden. As a high-ranking officer in the Kingdom, he was privy to God's plan and knew how to sever the relationship God had with Adam. If he couldn't be the king of the Kingdom of Heaven, he certainly would make sure he became the king of the Kingdom of Earth and knew exactly how to steal it from Adam.

Thus, it all began in the Kingdom of Heaven, but will end in the Kingdom of Earth when Christ returns to win the war against Lucifer. In the meantime, we are children caught in the crossfire and our salvation is dependent upon which king we believe.

2

Death of the Spirit

God created Adam so He would have children, made like Himself of the Spirit. He clothed him in a body and gave him a soul, or free will to think, make decisions, and experience emotions. He didn't want robots that acted on command, but living beings who would love Him as their Father by choice. Because God and His Kingdom are Spirit, man is made a spirit being. Therefore, God's relationship with Adam and his wife, Eve, is one of spirit though they had a physical body.

When God took dust from the earth and formed the physical shape of what we know as the human form, it was like a rag doll until God breathed into the nostrils giving life to the form. Not just life, but God put Himself within this man He named Adam. Because we know God is Love and God is Spirit, He made this man in His own image, His likeness, of the spirit. What this means is out of God's love, He fashioned man and put a spirit person inside the clay body, a replica of Himself.

Then God gave man a soul, free will. It is the soul that enables man to have his own thoughts. Without a free will, or free thinking, man would be mechanical in his application of life, like a computer that has to be given commands to function. The soul is what links the body and the spirit; it is the connector. The body can do nothing on its own, and the spirit can do nothing until it is awakened by a birth in Christ; therefore, it is the soul with its processing ability that governs man's humanistic behavior.

To destroy the relationship between God and Adam and steal the Kingdom of Earth, it required putting to death the spirit person of Adam. Adam was perfectly made, lived in a holy and perfect paradise, and had a very special relationship with God. God and Adam spent much time together and God was exceedingly pleased with His child, and Adam loved his Father. Lucifer, being an angelic being, knew how to kill Adam, spiritually. Just as he influenced one-third of the angels in the Kingdom of Heaven, he knew how to deceive Adam.

When Lucifer presented disharmony in the Kingdom of Heaven, God removed him. In Adam's disobedience to his Father, God removed Adam and Eve from the Garden. Sin cannot exist where holiness prevails, for sin will taint the purity and glory of the holy place.

It was the spirit person of the trinity of man that died when sin entered with Satan's lie. The body and soul of man remained, leaving Adam and Eve as carnal beings aware of their physical nakedness. They knew something had happened to them, for they were no longer spirit persons.

Adam and Eve lived their remaining days as carnal beings and not spirit persons. Adam lost his position as king, his paradise homeland, his privilege to walk in the Garden with God. His relationship changed, though

God continued to communicate with Adam, it wasn't the same.

Adam was rich and became poor because he believed a lie which brought a curse upon himself and every generation born after him. The second Adam, Christ, was rich and became poor, leaving His throne in the Kingdom of Heaven and came to Earth to remove the curse, cleanse the sin, and reconcile man in a spirit birth back to God, Almighty King. The spirit person of man died by the first Adam and is reborn in the second Adam.

We are all born with the curse of sin into a corrupt world with a ruler who's sole ambition is to separate us from knowing our Almighty King, the One who gave us life. It is Satan's objective to prevent the generations of children since Adam from ever being reborn to their spirit person because it reunites them to God. The Word, the Son of God, the second Adam, Christ, left His throne and dwelt among the people on Earth for a short time to teach them of their heavenly Father, One who loves them.

The Word of God is the very essence of what Satan doesn't want anyone to have knowledge of, so he has devised a method to defraud God's truth by using God's own Words against Him. Presently, it is a warfare of words, but in Christ's second coming, He will destroy Lucifer by locking him in the bottomless pit, forever. Then He will claim all the saints, the children, who were once lost to the Father, those who believe in His Son.

How does Satan accomplish such an enormous task of deflecting so many people from the knowledge of God? Actually, the answer is very simple and can be summed up with one word, religion. What is the meaning of religion, exactly? Religion is a pursuit or interest to which someone ascribes supreme importance; a particular system of faith and worship. Though God is of supreme importance, He is not a system. God is not a religion, nor did Christ come to Earth to teach a religion.

Simply put, man could not agree on what God's Word meant; therefore, in their disgruntled stance, the people split and created their own doctrine with each holding themselves to have the only true knowledge of God. This has perpetuated throughout the generations, and why there are numerous doctrines being taught in various congregations today. Satan devised it and man accepts it.

Consequently, Christians believe they have a commodity on the knowledge of God no matter which doctrine they are associated with; however, it is the believers who are gravely deceived. What does God say? *That your faith should not stand in the wisdom of men, but in the power of God.* 1 Corinthians 2:5 Satan wants you to be following a false doctrine, a false belief, because it will keep you from a relationship with God.

We become prideful in our belief and trust only our own understanding. However, unless you are being taught by the tutor whom God has given to you, beware. Caution is needed when you hear the gospel of Christ being taught to make certain it confirms what the Holy Spirit, the *Spirit of Truth*, teaches.

In many churches today, only a half-truth is being preached and not the truth that Christ taught when He was on Earth; the true gospel of Christ. This subtle but profound implementation of lies succinctly interjected along with truth makes the Word of God to no affect in the believer's life. This is a hard concept for many to grasp, but ponder on this for a moment.

If you were a world leader and you wanted to keep every person under your influence, how would you best accomplish such a task? You would present a doctrine that all will accept and follow, willingly. Accepting that you may not be holding to a doctrine that is the complete truth is hard for most to consider, and more so, if you have held to one understanding your entire life.

Can you imagine what it must have been like for the people across the land to hear of a Messiah, Jesus, teaching of an Almighty King, a God they had never heard of before? Jesus taught to as many as would listen all about the Kingdom of Heaven and of a Father who loved them. How foreign that must have been to them. And the Pharisees were determined to keep the people in bondage to their belief. Remember, it was Satan who influenced Judas Iscariot to betray Jesus, having him killed to destroy His teaching the people about God.

Today, we are a people no different than the Israelites who didn't realize in their present day life of slavery what they were missing until they were removed by a loving and merciful God. Even then, they couldn't accept a King who loved them and would care for them. Many believe they have the knowledge of God's Word without realizing they have been led astray. Satan doesn't need to exert any wiles to tangle the life of an unbeliever, for they have chosen to not accept God. He must keep the ones who seek God from ever having a relationship with Him.

It is imperative to understand there are two kingdoms, two kings, two principles in place with two very different outcomes for your life; and yes, it begins the day you were born. You were branded upon birth by Satan, and he claims ownership of you. The only way to escape his corruption is to be born out of it, figuratively and literally, through Christ.

You have to be born into the spirit person to remove the curses of bondage that holds you captive. It must be one or the other, for the two gods are not joining forces to give you a great life. God and Satan are not teaming up for your benefit; however, you do have the free will to choose. Choose wisely, for it does affect your life today and forever.

3

Birth of the Spirit

We know we are born spirit from the Spirit of God. We also understand the death of the spirit in man was through Adam. To give birth to the spirit person within man, it requires the second Adam, Jesus. Born of the flesh, our spirit is asleep, unresponsive until quickened, or awakened by Christ with His Spirit.

To best illustrate the significance of our spirit person, imagine a human being with a zipper running down the front likened to a scuba diving suit that fits like a second skin; however, in this scenario, you are unzipping the body like a *flesh* suit and a spirit person steps out and the suit falls to the ground. As you step out of the bodysuit, you find yourself invisible, and yet, you know that you are a living being. This is the real you, meant for God. You are a spirit person living in a bodysuit of flesh, blood, and bones which is your exterior shell to house the spirit you.

You are born with a physical body into a natural world: however, your body houses your spirit person. Can you better envision that the spirit person inside you is a real person? And it is this spirit being that God is waiting to be awakened for Himself, so that you can be His child. Are you beginning to grasp why it is imperative to give birth to your spirit if you want to be with the Father, reconciled and reconnected to Him?

Adam was created a spirit person, given a flesh body but lived as a spirit being, perfect before God in the Garden. You are born with a physical body living in a corrupt world with a spirit person waiting to be born into the Kingdom of Heaven, back to the Garden of Eden. Adam was uncorrupted but became corrupt. You are born corrupt and must be reborn to become un-corrupted.

Adam's spirit person died because of sin and he became carnal. Likewise, you must die to your carnality or sin, so that you may be born of the spirit. Why is this so important? Without this transition, it is impossible to be a child of God. His Kingdom is of the Spirit. Your physical body is tainted with sin and is of the natural world.

It's necessary to dissect the trinity of man in order to understand the significance of each life: a worldly life driven by fleshly desires, or a spiritual life directed by the precepts of God. Is your soul persuaded by the flesh, or by the spirit? It is easy to accept the things of the world as the real deal, but God tells us they are temporal and will return to the earth. The flesh of man will die, decay, and become ashes of the earth from where he came.

God made man to live forever, but He could only do that in the spirit. Only the spirit of man can have the hope of an eternal life, and I say hope because you have to use your free will to choose to awaken the spirit person within you. Until the time when Christ returns and we are resurrected into our new bodies (without blood) and live with Christ as our King, it is the spirit of man Christ came to Earth to reconnect to the Spirit Father within His Spirit Kingdom.

It is Christ's Spirit who gives you this spiritual birth. This was the purpose of the *Word* coming to Earth and living as a man, taking our punishment, dying in our place that we may live forever in a spiritual Kingdom. It can only be accomplished in the spirit realm.

To give birth to your spirit person, you must accept Christ. It is His Spirit entwined with your spirit that awakens your spirit from sleep. In Christ, you are alive and ready to live spiritually. So what happens when your spirit is awakened with no memory to draw from? It is fresh, new, untouched, pure and holy, righteous and ready for the Father's instructions. However, you can have your spirit quickened, and yet, never learn to live a spirit life.

Many believers never get beyond this point. As such, they accept Christ and the gift of salvation and no more. Why? They simply haven't been taught in their de-nominational congregations how to live a spirit-oriented life. As such, they remain without the privileges and pleasures of living within God's Kingdom, which begins the moment you are born into it.

The blessings, gifts, and supernatural power is not available to them which is why so many aren't receiving a healing, miracles, and prosperity. If you receive Christ simply for salvation, you miss everything the Father has within His Kingdom for you, today.

As a newborn spirit person, God instructs you to step out of the world, be not conformed to the world and its ways, and learn to live a spiritual life under the principles of His Kingdom. *And be not conformed to this world: but be ye transformed by the renewing of your mind, that ye may prove what is that good, and acceptable, and perfect, will of God.* Romans 12:2

Christ has freed you from the bondage of the corruption of this earthen world, freed you from Satan's strongholds, and provided you passage into the Father's Kingdom. It is the spirit person only that connects to God because God is Spirit, Christ is Spirit, the Holy Ghost is Spirit, and the Kingdom of Heaven is Spirit. The obvious question to ask yourself is are you living a spirit-filled and spirit-led life receiving the gifts and power available to you from the Father?

Nothing is more important than being born into the Kingdom of Heaven, having an intimate relationship with your heavenly Father, and living with all the magnificent provisions He has for you, His child. He wants to give you the storehouse of treasures that were meant to help you and your family today and every day you remain in this earthen world.

Remember, as a spirit person you rely and receive of God, not of the world. You are separate from the world and with the Holy Spirit living in your heart and your soul is focused on the Kingdom of Heaven, all things are possible because God set forth His Kingdom this way, for you.

4

Freedom of a Free Will

Being a God of love, He gave every person, including angels, a free will that all would praise and worship Him as their Almighty King. However, man has an advantage over the angels, for we are His most precious children. God wanted children who would freely come to Him, for He will not coerce anyone to be His child.

Man's expression of his free will is evident through his soul and witnessed in his personality. Each person is responsible to use their free will for the sole purpose of acknowledging and accepting the truth of God's Word and choosing to be born a spirit person into the Kingdom of Heaven. *Accept, I beseech thee, the free will offerings of my mouth, O Lord, and teach me thy judgements.* Psalm 119:108 It is a soulful conscious thought to depart from the influences of this earthen world and be joined in Christ for the Father.

When studying the semantics of the two kingdoms, their rulers, inhabitants, principles and power, clarity is necessary to better understand God's creation, and how a free will can be manipulated if you are not grounded and living under the precepts of the Kingdom of

Heaven. Even the angels in the Kingdom who were with God could be persuaded to oppose Him. If angels who know firsthand His Almighty presence can be influenced, how much more likely that we humans can be deceived? If we begin at the most elementary point, it becomes an objective learning curve in the realization of what can go wrong.

There are different laws, or precepts that govern each of the kingdoms. It is very important to understand the difference because it affects the outcome of your life. In God's Kingdom, man has a relationship with God as the Father just as it was with Adam in the Garden.

God makes available for His children, who come to Him, a storehouse of treasures that are generously supplied for your earthen life. Some believe these gifts are for our future in the Kingdom of Peace, or what we refer to as the Millennium, the one-thousand year reign of Christ before the New Jerusalem. However, living in our new bodies with Christ, our King, we will not need these gifts. They are meant for this earthen life as the Father provides and protects His children from the corruption of a fallen world.

Born of the spirit in Christ entitles you to the privileges of all the things within the Spirit Kingdom. You remain physically residing in this earthen world, but you now belong to the Kingdom of Heaven. All your needs are met and supplied by the spirit world.

There is heavenly supernatural power to be obtained for healing, miracles, prosperity; for all things. God withholds nothing from His children who trust in Him. However, in the Kingdom of Earth in which you are born into, Satan rules and his intent is to keep you from knowing God and receiving His gifts. He can only give you misery, heartache, disease, and death. No good comes from Lucifer.

We have been so indoctrinated with false information passed on throughout the generations, especially about obeying the Mosaic Law, which is Satan's plan of deception, that it is very difficult for people to open their mind to accept something different from what they have always known.

Though the Ten Commandments, the Law of Moses, is holy because it comes from a holy God, it was meant for a duration of time, for the Jews, before the Son of God brought a new covenant for all the people, Jews and Gentiles. One way that Satan can keep people in bondage and away from God is to keep them believing they are still under the law.

In following the law, is to not accept the new testament in Christ and all that He has done at the Cross. Christ fulfilled the law by taking the sins of the world upon Himself. In turn, He gives us His righteousness and grace. *For the law was given by Moses, but grace and truth came by Jesus Christ.* John 1:17 No truth is found in the law because righteousness is not of the law.

Satan has done an exceptional job of deceiving the people. Repentance is a changing of the mind, a turning away from one source of belief or understanding to another. Isn't that exactly what we are required to do when we choose to accept Christ as our mediator, who will give us a rebirth into the Kingdom of Heaven? Following the law will not gain you entrance into Heaven.

Let's begin with the very first use of your free will. You come into this Kingdom called Earth as a person born with a curse on your life and a sin nature. You had no choice, no say, regarding your birth into the Kingdom of Earth; however, you do have a say to be born into God's Kingdom of Heaven. This alone is a significant realization each person should come to, the use of your free will. You can spend your entire life in sin, in a corrupt world, and accept this is all there is to life: basically, you live and die...the end. You have used your free will to not believe in another kingdom. Or somewhere in maturation, you learn there is another god, another kingdom, another life...and its eternal.

From a child's perspective, you may have been taught through your parents, grandparents, or others a doctrine about a God who lives in a heavenly Kingdom; a God who loves you. Initially, as an adolescent, your informational resource comes from these sources, so your knowledge is limited to their understanding.

You may go to church because they take you there, and you believe what they tell you to believe, it's simple and easy. This is typical throughout the generations. We fall back on others and what they believe rather than seeking the truth for ourselves. Caution must be exercised for the very idea should they be incorrect, and you choose to hold to a false doctrine, it does affect your relationship, or lack thereof, with God. God expects you to learn from the teacher He gives, not rely on man's interpretation.

Whatever age you are until you make the choice to accept Christ as your redeemer and be born into the Kingdom of Heaven, you are still living as an unbeliever. No one can choose God for you, and you alone must decide to learn from God's tutor.

However, let's say a time comes in your adult life,

having heard of a heavenly Father, you decide to accept the God you've heard so much about. Perhaps due to circumstances, you finally come to a crossroad where you want a relationship with God, motivated to seek Him and His Kingdom. What happens next? It must be said that this is a monumental and life-altering *rite of passage*, literally, that most are clueless as to how to make the transition from living a life of unbelief to one of pure trust and faith in God. Once you grasp the magnitude, it will change your life forever as it's meant to do.

The problem remains that even for those who believe in Christ and have repented of their sins, and are now born into the Kingdom of Heaven, remain uneducated in how to live within this new Kingdom, while physically remaining in the earthen one. Satan is still at work to derail you from the presence of God. In fact, he will work more diligently to prevent you from having a relationship with Him.

It should be your desire to learn the principles that govern God's Kingdom, to want to know about your Father, the One you never knew but has always loved you from afar. God gives you an instruction book, the Bible, detailing His truths along with a personal tutor, the Holy Spirit, to teach you all things of His Kingdom. Remaining ignorant will leave you without His blessings and provisions.

Satan isn't overtly concerned by you calling yourself a believer, because he can still keep you in bondage if you remain believing a false doctrine about God. The summation is this: you can believe in God, praise Him in worship, and yet, be lead astray from a relationship with Him. Something to seriously ponder.

What you believe is where your trust lies, and if not grounded in the truth taught by the Holy Spirit, there's a problem that needs to be rectified. If you want healing, need a miracle, and prosperity in this lifetime, God has provided this through the gifts and power of the Holy Spirit.

We are to learn from the Holy Spirit who is specifically sent to teach all things concerning the Father's Kingdom. Then when we hear, or read of God's Word, we instinctively know it to be a truth or a lie, for the Spirit of Truth testifies of God's Word.

5

Righteousness or Self-Righteousness

Lucifer exerted a self-righteous behavior within the Kingdom of Heaven believing himself equal to the Almighty King. Interesting how man has the same inherent characteristics of Lucifer, meaning that everything that occurred to Adam which has been passed down through the generations is of Lucifer's traits. Adam was a means by which Satan could continue his rebellion against God through the man God created for Himself. Satan is on the same course to deceive and destroy the people whom God intended to be His children.

Satan easily manipulated Adam through his soul. God did not abandon Adam; however, he was left on his own cognizance to make a living off the land he once governed. Adam was no longer a spirit person living in the Garden, but now a carnal being working for his livelihood.

Not only was Satan's objective to steal Adam's position of authority, but to remove Adam and the subsequent children from God. This continues to be his strategy today. Separated from God, we are without righteousness and righteousness is required in God's

Kingdom. We must be without sin. *For as by one man's disobedience many were made sinners, so by the obedience of one shall many be made righteous.* Romans 5:19 Righteousness is of God and self-righteousness is of Satan; therefore, we are born with a self-righteous trait. However, reborn to the spirit person we are in Christ, righteousness is given as a gift. *For he hath made him to be sin for us, who knew no sin; that we might be made the righteousness of God in him.* 2 Corinthians 5:21 There is only one way to obtain righteousness and that is through Christ.

As Satan rules his Kingdom with a roaming eye, he is making sure that the people remain self-righteous, self-absorbed, self-conscious, and self-occupied. When you are self-absorbed, you are not thinking of anyone but yourself. Your thoughts and actions reflect a lifestyle consumed by your wants and desires. *Now about the midst of the feast Jesus went into the temple, and taught. And the Jews marveled, saying, How knoweth this man letters, having never learned? Jesus answered them, and said, My doctrine is not mine, but his that sent me. If any man will do his will, he shall know of the doctrine, whether it be of God or whether I speak of myself. He that speaketh of himself seeketh his own glory; but he that seeketh his glory that sent him, the same is true, and no unrighteousness is in him.* John 7:14-18

We are certainly a society so completely self-absorbed to the point where *selfie* is an applicable term. We spend an enormous amount of time involved in what we believe will bring us pleasure and happiness. As long as we remain self-focused, we maintain a self-righteous behavior; thus, believing only in ourselves and at best those around us. The focus is not on God; therefore, our dependency is not on Him.

It is natural to turn to man for resolutions, encouragement, and validation because trust is based on self-righteousness and not righteousness. Meaning, we instinctively put our trust and faith in man instead of God. We place faith in what we see and not in the unseen, which is the very opposite of what God instructs.

The reality for a spirit-led person should be the spiritual realm. Our faith and trust is in our Almighty King, our heavenly Father. Relying on someone for comfort in a crisis is human nature, but the dependency for a resolution should always come from the Father. He is the One we turn to in time of need.

A righteous person, born of the spirit in Christ for the Father, knows to put his faith in all things of the Kingdom of Heaven. A self-righteous person only knows the ways of the kingdom he was born into. It has never been a matter of falling from righteousness because we aren't born righteous to begin with. However, we accept our righteousness in Christ and in doing so choose to discard our selfish and singleminded way of thinking, trusting the One who is greater than ourselves.

If you want to be a righteous person and live a righteous life, there is only one way and one person whereby this is possible, and His name is Yeshua (Hebrew) translated to Greek (Iesous) to Latin (Iesus), to English, Jesus. In the Kingdom of Heaven, He is known as the *Word*; however, when the *Word* left His throne and came to Earth and became flesh, a human being, He is given an earthen name of Hebrew descent. He is also called Yahweh which means *Lord our Savior;* and

Jehovah, the Lord. And the Word was made flesh, and dwelt among us, (and we beheld his glory, the glory as of the only begotten of the Father,) full of grace and truth. John 1:14

The second person of the trinity of God, the *Word,* the Son of God takes the sins of the world and gives the gift of righteousness. When Jesus died on the Cross, we also died with Him, figuratively. *Therefore we are buried with him by baptism into death: that like as Christ was raised up from the dead by the glory of the Father, even so we also should walk in newness of life. For if we have been planted together in the likeness of his death, we shall be also in the likeness of his resurrection: Knowing this, that our old man is crucified with him, that the body of sin might be destroyed, that henceforth we should not serve sin. For he that is dead is freed from sin. Now if we be dead with Christ, we believe that we shall also live with him.* Romans 6:4-8

It is impossible to be righteous of your own accord because you are born a sinner with a corrupt nature, it's inherent to who you are having inherited the trait from Adam. You receive your righteousness solely in Christ as a gift. It isn't something to be earned. An exchange occurs whereby Jesus receives your sins and iniquities and you receive His righteousness.

Jesus did no sin and had no sin in Him, but He took your place and died for you. You have no righteousness or holiness in you, but you take His righteousness and holiness. There is a transformation between a holy God and sinful man. You are now joint-heirs in Christ for everything God desires to give you.

Why is righteousness so important? To answer this question, we need to once again look at the two kingdom's principles. One functions in self-righteous-ness, while the other is governed in righteousness. Self-righteousness will never get you close to God even if you are a born-again believer. *He that speaketh of himself seeketh his own glory: but he that seeketh his glory that sent him, that the same is true, and no unrighteousness is in him.* John 7:18

To have a relationship with the Father, we have to be clothed in righteousness, meaning our covering of sins and transgressions must be removed. We know this is done through the cleansing blood of Christ when he shed His blood at Calvary. No man on this earth can claim a righteous life but through Christ. Just as Adam lived in righteousness in the Garden, a righteousness given by God, but once he sinned, righteousness was removed. Sin dwelt in him and self-righteousness is the outflowing behavior.

The importance of righteousness simply stated is that it is the only way to the Kingdom of Heaven. *Righteousness and justice are the foundation of Your throne; Mercy and truth go before Your face.* Psalm 89:14 Christ fulfilled all at the Cross and stated, *It is Finished.* The plan God has for the people, Jews and Gentiles, is now done. It becomes a matter of using our free will to accept what was set forth at the foundation of Creation by God and completed by the Son.

The precepts that govern man have already been established at Creation; however, we need to under-stand what they are and live by them if we expect to enter God's Almighty Kingdom. *For they being ignorant of God's righteousness, and going about to establish their own righteousness, have not submitted themselves unto the righteousness of God.* Romans 10:3

We cannot be self-righteous and righteous at the same time. God will not permit it. Self-righteousness is a sin that cannot be allowed in His holy place just as it was not allowed in the Garden of Eden. The evidence is Lucifer's display of self-righteousness and it cost him removal from the Kingdom of Heaven. Righteousness no longer existed for Adam once he sinned, and it cost him removal from the Garden.

You live in an unrighteous world, and if you want to obtain righteousness, you have to shed the self-righteous behavior and take on the righteousness given in Christ. He clothes you in His righteousness that you may be presentable before God. *For if by one man's offence death reigned by one; much more they which receive abundance of grace and of the gift of righteousness shall reign in life by one, Jesus Christ.* Romans 5:17 Remember, righteousness is a gift. It cannot be earned by doing good deeds.

After receiving your spirit birth in Christ and accepting His gift of righteousness, you are presentable for a relationship with the Father. However, holding onto self-righteousness as Satan would have you do prevents you from getting close to God. When you accept Christ as your Lord and Savior, your iniquities and curses are no more. Bondage to sin has been nailed to the Cross, and you are now robed in righteousness, pure and holy for the Father.

6

Son of God, Son of Man

In the beginning within the Kingdom of Heaven, there was God, the Word, and the Holy Ghost. God is all three, and yet, gives Himself in three personages for man. When God created man, Adam, He became a Father to Adam. When Adam became a prodigal son, God sent the *Word* to become His beloved Son, the second Adam.

This Son, who is perfectly holy and perfectly righteous, would reconcile the generations of people born from the seed of the first Adam. We are born into the natural world from the first Adam (a physical birth) and born into the spirit Kingdom through the second Adam (spirit birth) to be the children of God.

The *Word* came to Earth, born of flesh, and became a man. The *Word* took on the names *Son of God* and *Son of Man*. Meaning, He is both which depicts He is all God and all man. God from the Spirit Kingdom and man for the earthen Kingdom. *Whosoever shall confess that Jesus is the <u>Son of God</u>, God dwelleth in him, and he in God.* 1 John 4:15 Also, *The beginning of the gospel of Jesus Christ, the <u>Son of God</u>.* Mark 1:1 And, *But that ye may know that the <u>Son of man</u> hath power on* *earth to forgive sins.* Matthew 9:6 Also, *For the <u>Son of</u> <u>man</u> is Lord even of the sabbath day.* Matthew 12:8 There are numerous Scriptures depicting the role of Christ as both Son of God and Son of Man. It is necessary to distinguish between the personages, and how they are meant for man's life.

We know the *Word* as Jesus Christ. However, born of Jewish parents, His Hebrew name is Yeshua. Yeshua translated from Hebrew to Greek to Latin to English gives us the name Jesus. The trinity of God, the Word, and the Holy Ghost became the Father, the Son, and the Holy Spirit. The distinction is the Kingdom of Heaven without man, and the Kingdom of Earth with man. Before there was Adam (man) there was no personage of the Father and the Son.

Though the second Adam was before the first Adam (man), it wasn't until the fall of the first Adam that the second Adam became the Son of God, literally. It was already preplanned by God at His Creation what would be required for man. Therefore, the second person of the trinity of God, the Word, became the Son of God and also the Son of Man.

The King came down from His throne to become human and live among the people to take back what Lucifer stole in the Garden of Eden and continues to steal today…if you allow him. Christ came as the *Word,* as the *Son of God,* and became the *Son of Man* when born of flesh. However, in His appearance on earth, He did not do away with Satan, not yet, because of the free will given to man.

The Son of God came to teach man about the One, Almighty King in the Kingdom of Heaven, and allowing man to choose his god. God put a timeframe for man's existence, six-thousand years, with the final one-thousand years with Christ as our King in the Kingdom of Peace. When the time comes, it will be the Son of God who will destroy Lucifer, but it was the Son of Man who died on the Cross for man. Sin had to be dealt with in the flesh.

While Christ was on Earth, He had many names, more than fifty recorded in the Scriptures. Perhaps the most significant are the *Word,* the *Living Water*, the *Bread of Life, the Light of the World,* the *Prince of Peace, the Lamb of God*, and the *Good Shepherd*, for each tells of what He gives to man. The King came to Earth and served the people. *Even as the <u>Son of man</u> came not to be ministered unto, but to minister, and to give his life a ransom for many.* Matthew 20:28 We've been taught such a watered-down version that we completely miss the magnitude of His mission.

We accept Christ as the Son of God, that He died on the Cross for our sins and gives us salvation (eternal life). This is where the teaching ends in most traditional doctrines. Some denominations will mention that you receive the gift of the Holy Spirit when you repent and accept Jesus as your Lord and Savior, but there is no explanation of how to apply this most precious gift and why you are given Him in the first place. There is much to what Christ has done and prepared for man's life.

If you truly knew what has been given to you through the Son of God and the Son of Man, Christ Himself, you would be awe struck, not just amazed, but in awe! It should surely humble you to your knees. And to think that it was all for you.

All things are given on the authority of Christ who is now seated at the right hand of the Father in the Kingdom of Heaven. God gave ownership to His Son, and the Son gives you Kingdom privileges and power. *Jesus knowing that the Father had given all things into his hands, and that he was come from God, and went to God.* John 13:3

God in the personages of the Father, the Son, and the Holy Spirit is for the purpose of giving to you, serving you, protecting and providing for you. Notice the Father <u>gives</u>, the Son <u>serves</u>, and the Holy Spirit <u>provides</u>. Jesus served the people while on Earth and continues to serve you now in Heaven. Without this understanding of how God set forth His Kingdom, you will surely miss His provisions.

Your heavenly gifts are being stolen like a thief in the night without your knowledge or consent. Remember, this is a spiritual battle, and Satan runs interference and literally blocks you from knowing the truth of God's Kingdom and receiving His treasures by keeping you ignorant.

In the Old Testament, God removed the people from slavery and told them He was their God who loved them and would provide and care for them, give them a homeland of riches and fertile land; and yet, they refused by default of worshipping other gods. In fact, they were afraid of God and asked Moses to be their spokesperson, but God had already planned for Moses to be the mediator making a covenant with him for the people.

It wasn't until after forty years and the generation died off, that their children were given the same promise of a land to inhabit, the one promised to their fathers. After Moses death, Joshua led them to their new homeland.

For four-thousand years, God dealt with the people both Jews and Gentiles as Satan waged war to deter the people from the knowledge of Him. Lucifer was the king of the Kingdom of Earth and diligently worked then and now to place obstacles in the people's path, so they would stumble in knowledge, wisdom, and the truth of the Almighty King. It was only a matter of time when God would need to leave His throne and come to Earth to deal with the problem of Satan. So God came as the Son of God and the Son of Man.

During the time that Jesus was on Earth, He told His disciples: *Jesus saith unto him, Have I been so long time with you, and yet hast thou not known me, Philip? he that hath seen me hath seen the Father; and how sayest thou then, Shew us the Father?* John 14:9

Christ placed Himself in a position to gather the lost people to the Father. He spent His time teaching of God and His Kingdom. Miracles and healing revealed to them He was who He said He was and came from a Kingdom they had yet to know and that an eternal life awaited those who believed in Him.

When Jesus' work was finished and He returned to His throne, He anointed His disciples to continue His teachings. They were given supernatural Kingdom power through the third person of the trinity, the Holy Spirit, to continue performing miracles, healing, and raise the dead. Today, He gives you the same power.

There are many who teach *of* God but not *about* Him. They speak *of* Christ, but not *about* His works and His truths. How can you ask Him anything, if you don't know the person you are asking of? How can you receive, if you don't understand the methodology of where to begin? It's necessary to be very reflective of this thought because everything lies within the answer to these two questions. If you don't know who, and you don't know what, how can you receive?

You may think your faith rests in Christ, and yet, perhaps living under the influences of another, un-beknownst. This would be a good time to meditate on God's Word and be assured.

7

A Body for the Son of God

We know that man is made in the image of God who is Spirit and because God has a soul He also gave man a soul as we are made in His complete likeness. *And I will be a tabernacle among you: and my soul shall not abhor you. And I will walk among you, and will be your God, and ye shall be my people."* Leviticus 26:11-12 God created man as He is; therefore, so are we.

Though God does not have a physical body, it was necessary to design man with a flesh body as it would be required for the *Word* to live among the people. The body is the earthen home for the *Word (the Word became flesh and dwelt among us)* and for the *Comforter*, the Holy Spirit. Our body becomes the temple of God for His earthen purpose. *What? know ye not that your body is the temple of the Holy Ghost which is in you, which ye have of God, and ye are not your own?* 1 Corinthians 6:19 God, Himself, came to Earth through the medium of the physical body. To those born in Christ's Spirit, you have the Son of God (Christ) and the Spirit of God (Holy Spirit) within you.

Have you ever wondered why a trinity? For example,

God, the Word, and the Holy Ghost; the Father, the Son, and the Holy Spirit; the Word, the Son of God, and the Son of Man; man with a body, soul, and spirit; and the Kingdom functions with mercy, grace, and faith. And remember the three archangels, Michael, Gabriel, and Lucifer. Also, the three important mountains where God and Christ appear: Mount Sinai, Mount Zion, and Mount of Olives.

Then we have events that occur in three days. God told Moses to have the people ready themselves and bring them to Mount Sinai in three days, Saul (Paul) was blinded for three days, Peter denied Jesus three times, Yeshua (Jesus) was missing for three days when his parents found Him in a synagogue at the age of twelve, Satan tempted Christ three times in the wilderness, Jesus brought three men to the mountaintop to be witnesses (Peter, James, and John), Jonah stayed in the belly of the whale for three days, and Christ was re-surrected on the third day. Even the conflict with God, Lucifer, and Adam; and now with God, Satan, and man.

The prodigal son was given a robe, a ring, and sandals for his feet. We are instructed to not follow the ways of the world as it is defined in three concepts: lust of the eyes, lust of the flesh, and pride of life. However, we hold strong in faith, trust, and belief. This is not a coincidence, for nothing in God's plan is without a purpose. If you study the trinity, you will discover each independent entity has a distinct reason for man. There are numerous occasions within the Scriptures.

We know God's number seven represents perfection and completion as reflected in His seven days of Creation, whereby we base the Hebrew (lunar) and Gregorian (sun) calendar of seven days in a week. There will be seven years of tribulation during the last days of man's existence on Earth; seven places on Christ's body where He shed blood during His crucifixion, the seven final words spoken by Jesus before He gave up the Ghost; and God made seven specific covenants with man. There is also a seventh day sabbath, seven year sabbath, and a seven times seven year sabbath (for the Jewish populous under the old covenant). Also, there are seven feasts celebrated by the Israelites (Jews) for the acknowledgement of Christ.

It is noteworthy of the number three reflecting God's work, while the number seven is His holiness. It is worth the study of the numbers within the Scriptures, for each has an importance in God's plan. Therefore, learning of the numbers three, five, six, seven, ten, twelve, forty, and fifty gives you an account for the timing of events. Nothing of God's Creation is without significance; a plan which is recognized with a mathematical equivalence. To everything God created there is a numbering system in place, a timeline.

It's amazing when you see each aspect of how God created and designed His Kingdom and prepared everything to be man's homeland. Adam lived in a paradise in the Kingdom God fashioned for him. God had a specific land promised to the Israelites, a homeland; and God has prepared mansions within the Kingdom for His children. *In my Father's house are many mansions: if it were not so, I would have told you. I go to prepare a place for you.* John 14:2

Let's take a look at the reason for man to have three components: a body, a soul, and a spirit. We know that man's spirit is made in the image of God and made for the Spirit Kingdom. We also know that in order to use the gift of a free will, we need a soul just as God has a soul. It is an outward expression of our personality and behavior. But why the body?

Before He created Adam from the Earth, there was no body in the Kingdom of Heaven. Angels were spirit beings, Lucifer was an archangel and remains today a spirit being. If all the Kingdom of Heaven is Spirit; God, the Word, the Holy Ghost and the angels, why change the mold of His creation to now include a physical form? It is a question to ponder, and the answer will surprise you. It is complex, and yet, simple once you begin to see the relevance.

God knew that Lucifer would defy Him, Adam would be disobedient, and man would betray Him. He created all things and set forth His plan whereas nothing will ever need to be altered or changed. God could have easily created Adam just as He created the angels with a free will and a spirit being, but no body. So the question is basic: why a physical form? There are two reasons.

Should God have created everything spiritual, angels and man, there would be no distinction between the two. Angels are servants and man His children, yet all would look the same. Our physical body distinguishes us to be His children, and when this earthen body returns to the dust of the earth from where it came, we are given a new body, physical in form but without blood, where we live eternally with the Father and His Son.

However, there is much more. Because God wanted children in His Kingdom and for them to be separate from His angelic beings, He fashioned man with his own unique design. He gave man a spirit within the body to be awakened only by His Son. It was planned for man to have a body and soul with a spirit.

Born with a physical body into a natural world is temporal; however, born in spirit we receive a new body that lives forever without aging and disease. One made of the earth for the Kingdom of Earth, and one of the spirit for the Kingdom of Heaven. One is temporary and the other eternal. To answer this, we have to go back to Adam. Remember, Adam and Eve lived and communicated with God daily as spirit persons, yet they had a body that they weren't aware of until they sinned.

Today it is the opposite, you have a physical body that you are aware of; however, you are a spirit person waiting to be born into the Kingdom. Your life should not be about the physical but about the spirit person; the person meant for an eternal life. Having a physical body with blood on Earth and without blood in Heaven visually identifies you as children of the Father.

The second reason for a body for man is for His Son, Jesus. God's plan required an earthen vessel to house His Spirit for the duration of time He would be on Earth as Christ. *Jesus saith unto him, I am the way, the truth, and the life: no man cometh unto the Father, but by me. John 14:6* It was necessary for man to see and witness the miracles on their level as a human being. An invisible spiritual being wouldn't be able to accomplish this task. It's difficult for many today to believe in the unseen, so how much more difficult would it have been for those who had not been exposed to the gospel of Christ?

So the second person of the trinity, the Word became the Son of God whereby He maintains His deity as King, and came to Earth and became the Son of Man, born of the flesh. God became a human being in Christ to be able to be among the people and teach them of Himself and His Kingdom. Remember, when God took the Israelites from Egypt, and He came in a cloud and spoke to them, they could not see Him and were fearful. They only heard His voice.

Can you imagine it might be the same today? In reality, it makes sense to come to Earth as one of us, live among the people, and speak to them on their level. God needed a physical body to be born into, a physical body to bare the transgressions of the world, a physical body to be resurrected, and a physical body (without blood) to ascend to Heaven. God was born as Jesus, the Son of Man and it was the Son of Man who died on the Cross. We can see, once again, how God did this for man.

When Jesus arose from the dead, He didn't return to Heaven as an invisible spirit being, but had a physical body and showed His disciples that He was still in human form. He ascended to the Kingdom in a body as all God and all Man. Now when you are resurrected, it will also be a physical body, no blood, but you will be a spirit person just like Christ, in His image. It comes full circle for man as it was with Adam and Eve in the Garden. We enter our paradise as spirit beings in a physical form.

It becomes clearer to see the relevancy of the body when we grasp the reason for the trinity of man. Man was first created as Adam, the first Adam, made for Earth, but also for the second Adam, Jesus. We are the generations born of the first Adam, a physical birth for the Earth and born of the second Adam, Christ, for Heaven. The soul and the spirit are of God, the body was necessary as part of His plan for man, and also, for the Word to come to Earth as Christ.

But there's more. It goes even beyond man's physical existence, for the body becomes the temple of God in this earthen world. We are the vessel He uses to be the home of His Spirit, the Holy Spirit. So when Christ returned to the Kingdom, He sends the Holy Spirit, the third person of the trinity of God, to dwell in the heart of each believer. The Holy Spirit has many roles in your life, but know Him as the power of God.

Acknowledging the creation of man with the trinity of body (earth), spirit (God), and soul (man), you could technically say that upon your spirit birth and quickening of the Holy Spirit, your body is the home of the Son of God (His Spirit intertwined with your spirit) and the Spirit of God (Holy Spirit). *The Spirit itself beareth witness with our spirit, that we are the children of God.* Romans 8:16 Also, *That which is born of the flesh is flesh; and that which is born of the Spirit is spirit.* John 3:6 The most crucial question is this: what are you doing with such eminence at your disposal?

After Christ ascended back to His throne, it is man that God relies on to be the stewards to continue His work on Earth. First, the chosen disciples by God, and today with each believer. We are to hold to the truth of His Word and not be swayed by the influences of this earthen kingdom. As we know the soul to be our connection between the body and the spirit, we should use caution as to who or what influences our soul. Born of the flesh with an un-awakened spirit, you are naturally drawn to the earthen things. However, to live a spirit life, it is acquiring wisdom of the unseen, the spirit realm.

Always remain focused to the reality there are two worlds, earthen and spirit, operating parallel and each has a ruler, a king. And it is not the familiar, but the spirit kingdom we seek. It becomes a true repentance or changing of the mind to accept the spirit person within and allow your spirit to mature in the knowledge of God.

When you accept the spirit world, the Kingdom of our Almighty God, you remain for a duration in your physical body _in_ this earthen world, but you are no longer _of_ this world. *If ye were of the world, the world would love his own: but because ye are not of the world, but I have chosen you out of the world, therefore the world hateth you.* John 15:19 You can be born again and easily remain under the influences of the physical.

This is why it is vital to learn from the Spirit of Truth, the tutor God gives to you. God instructs us to not follow the rudiments of the world but to follow Him. *Beware lest any man spoil you through philosophy and vain deceit, after the tradition of men, after the rudiments of the world, and not after Christ.* Colossians 2:8

Living as a spirit person in a Spirit Kingdom gives you all the privileges and power as Christ had on Earth. It was the Holy Spirit that empowered Jesus to heal and perform miracles. He did none until He was baptized with the Holy Spirit descending upon Him like a dove from Heaven. After that, He had the Holy Spirit within Him to do all things. Even in the Old Testament, it was the Holy Spirit that descended to Earth for a purpose and then returned to the Kingdom.

Today, Christ gives you His authority and the gift of the Holy Spirit when you are born into God's Kingdom. The Spirit of Truth is within you to teach, guide, protect, and provide heavenly power for your earthen life. God took care of Adam and Eve in the Garden, the Israelites in the desert, and He does the same today for you.

Don't allow your soul to be persuaded by the king or god of this earthen world whose only ambition is to destroy you. Rise above all that is temporal and live a life for the Father in His majestic and Almighty Kingdom where He has prepared a place just for you, today and forever!

8

God's Mediators

There are two mediators, or administrators, of God's Word: Moses and Jesus. We know of Moses in the Old Testament, and Jesus in the New Testament. Moses was a servant of God and Jesus, God's Son.

God sought Moses out in the desert while attending sheep and presented Himself as a burning bush and spoke to Moses. Because God heard the groaning of the Israelites in slavery to King Pharaoh in Egypt and remembered His covenant with Abraham, He chose Moses to be the mediator for the people. Upon removing the people from bondage, God set forth that He would be their king and they would be His people. Moses was four hundred and thirty years after Abraham.

When Moses became the mediator between God and the Israelites, God told Moses to bring the people to Him at the bottom of Mount Sinai where He detailed the law along with the statutes and judgements. Afterwards, God called Moses up to the mountain and Moses spent forty days with God. Moses brought back to the camp the Ten Commandments, the law written on stone by the finger of God. Henceforth, the law was administered by Moses meant for the carnal man.

For the duration of Moses' life, one-hundred and twenty years, God continued conversing with Moses on the people's behalf. As God instructed Moses, Moses in turn informed the people. Moses was a watchdog over the Commandments which is perhaps why they are referred to as the Law of Moses, or the Mosaic Law.

The purpose of the law was to show man that he needed a savior for his unruly, unrighteous, and sinful behavior. The law reveals to man his faults and short-comings. The law was meant to bring man to the end of himself and show his need for a redeemer. The law cannot give man purification from sin. The law cannot give man righteousness. The law cannot give man eternal life. The law can only end in the finality of death. Break the law and the punishment is to die, no exceptions.

No man on earth can follow the law perfectly except for one, Christ, whereby no sin was found in Him. Christ took our place for the punishment of our sins. When we accept Christ, our sins along with the law that judges sin are dead on the Cross. However, to those who refuse to accept God and believe in His Son, they will be judged by the law whereby there is no eternal life for them. They have not been redeemed by the blood of the Lamb of God.

As sin prevailed, God sent His Son to be the true mediator bringing forth a new testament, a better covenant for all the people, both Jews and Gentiles. The first carnal law was written on a tablet of stone, a physical presence, while the new spiritual law is written in the heart of every believer, a spiritual presence. *This is the covenant that I will make with them after those days, saith the Lord, I will put my laws into their hearts, and in their minds will I write them; And their sins and iniquities will I remember no more.* Hebrews 10:16-17

Only Christ can redeem us from the sin and curse placed on each person through the fall of Adam from God's grace. Without the Word coming to Earth to save man from his sins, no one would be able to enter into the Kingdom of Heaven. *And for this cause he is the mediator of the new testament, that by means of death, for the redemption of the transgressions that were under the first testament, they which are called might receive the promise of eternal inheritance.* Hebrews 9:15

In these remaining two-thousand years since Christ's resurrection and return to the throne, we have a covenant with the Son of God. *For this is my blood of the new testament, which is shed for many for the remission of sins.* Matthew 26:28 Christ makes a new covenant of Himself with each person who chooses Him. *By so much was Jesus made a surety of a better testament.* Hebrews 7:22

God knew sin had to be dealt with. It was never intended that the law, the Commandments, would bring righteousness and/or salvation to man. God had already set forth in His Almighty plan a time for His Son. Take to heart the magnitude of what God has *given*, and His Son has *done* for you.

It is only by the mercy and grace of our Most High God that we are freed from the bondage of sin and curses. No judgement and punishment is placed on you, for it was all put on the Son who took your place for God's wrath against unrighteousness. In Christ, you are found not guilty and your transgressions are remembered no more. His blood shed for you is your eternal protection against the bondage of sin.

Acknowledge and hold dearly to the covenant you have with the Son of God. *For if that first covenant had been faultless, then should no place have been sought for the second. For finding fault with them, he saith, Behold, the days come, saith the Lord, when I will make a new covenant with the house of Israel and with the house of Judah: Not according to the covenant that I made with their fathers in the day when I took them by the hand to lead them out of the land of Egypt; because they continued not in my covenant, and I regarded them not, saith the Lord. For this is the covenant that I will make with the house of Israel after those days, saith the Lord; I will put my laws into their mind, and write them in their hearts: and I will be to them a God, and they shall be to me a people: And they shall not teach every man his neighbour, and every man his brother, saying, Know the Lord: for all shall know me, from the least to the greatest. For I will be merciful to their unrighteousness, and their sins and their iniquities will I remember no more.* Hebrews 8:7-12

Since the resurrection of Christ, we have been given a new mediator, no longer under the mediator, Moses, the servant, but the mediator, Christ, the Son. *For there is one God, and one mediator between God and men, the man Jesus Christ; Who gave himself a ransom for all, to be testified in due time.* Timothy 2:5-6

As believers in Christ, we need to separate the two mediators. In not doing so, becomes a rejection of all that the Son of God in becoming the Son of Man did on the Cross. It is not possible to live under both for the law and grace do not mix. We live under the grace given in Christ. *For the law was given by Moses, but grace and truth came by Jesus Christ.* John 1:17

There are doctrines teaching the obedience of the law, and if you accept such, then you are not living under the mediator, Jesus. Lucifer would like for you to remain under the law because you cannot receive anything of God through obedience to the law.

After His Son has come to be our new mediator, it is an abomination to God to remain under the mediator of Moses, for the Son fulfilled the first covenant. *In that he saith, a new covenant, he hath made the first old. Now that which decayeth and waxeth old is ready to vanish away.* Hebrews 8:13 Therefore, choosing to live under the Law of Moses inherently rejects the Son of God. All the promises, blessings, gifts, and eternal life in the Kingdom of Heaven come through the Son of God, not by the law.

Satan has a subtle but profoundly effective method of keeping you from the promises of the new covenant in Christ. Following the law, you are kept under the law, always aware of your sins and sin nature as you attempt to be obedient to ten commands.

Only in Christ are sins forgiven, washed by the blood of the Lamb of God, curses are removed by His broken body on the Cross, and upon His death and your acceptance of Him, you are robed in the righteousness given in Christ. God sees no sin in you because of the veil of His Son's blood.

It is imperative to know which mediator you are following, for they cannot be combined, ever. *But now we are delivered from the law, that being dead wherein we were held; that we should serve in newness of spirit, and not in the oldness of the letter.* Romans 7:6

In following the law, expect judgement with the outcome of death. Believe in the new covenant in Christ and receive life. *For then must he often have suffered since the foundation of the world: but now once in the end of the world hath he appeared to put away sin by the sacrifice of himself. And as it is appointed unto men once to die, but after this the judgment: So Christ was once offered to bear the sins of many; and unto them that look for him shall he appear the second time without sin unto salvation.* Hebrews 9:26-28

Can you see how following the servant gains you nothing in the Kingdom of Heaven? If the law could give man righteousness, there would have been no need for a new covenant. Paul states: *I do not frustrate the grace of God: for if righteousness come by the law, then Christ is dead in vain.* Galatians 2:21 Under one mediator, sin is acknowledged before man, while under the other mediator sin is removed from man.

Once again, we witness a tactic of Lucifer to keep man in bondage, away from the truth of the one true Almighty King.

9

Communion in Christ

When Christ returned to the Kingdom of Heaven, He didn't leave man empty-handed. He taught specific men to continue in His place, but it doesn't end there. If it did and once these men died, who would carry on hence-forth? His teaching would eventually die with them, and no one would know of God and His Kingdom.

God's divine plan included a means that all men would have equal opportunity to know Him. God selected individuals who were called prophets and told them what to write down. *As it is written in the prophets, Behold, I send my messenger before thy face, which shall prepare thy way before thee.* Mark 1:2 These writings are referred to as Scriptures and are first noted in the Torah (Hebrew), translated to Greek, and finally to our English Bible.

Christ referred to what had been written in His many references when questioned by the Pharisees, priests, and even His disciples. *But he answered and said, It is written, Man shall not live by bread alone, but by every word that proceedeth out of the mouth of God.* Matthew 4:4 Remember, Christ is the *Word* who manifested all

God's Creation. Thus, He is speaking to the people of Himself. Many times He would refer to: *It is written,* exemplifying what will always remain without change.

Another example is when Satan tempted Jesus right after Christ received the Holy Spirit and was in the wilderness for forty days. *Then saith Jesus unto him, Get thee hence, Satan: for <u>it is written</u>, Thou shalt worship the Lord thy God, and him only shalt thou serve.* Matthew 4:10 Christ was the Word, and the written word was of Him that the prophets spoke of; and thus, Jesus stated often, *It is written,* because He spoke of what God and Himself established at Creation.

Christ was the Son of Man, but He was also the Son of God in His holy deity. Therefore, nothing was without His knowledge and this is why He always replied: *It is written,* just as His last words were, *It is finished.*

So when His work in this earthen kingdom was finished and He returned to His throne, what did He leave for man? Our Messiah left Himself to anyone who believes in who He is and from where He came.

How was He able to leave Himself when we know He ascended back to the Kingdom? And, since this was nearly two-thousand years ago when He made an appearance on Earth, what do we have of Him today? We would naturally answer these questions by saying we have the Scriptures that teach of who He is. This is true; however, traditional studies have a tendency to focus on the name of Jesus rather than the personages of Son and of Man. To know Christ, it is necessary to see the two deities He presents for man.

He became the beloved Son of God and the sacrificial Son of Man. The Son of Man, His human person, who died on the Cross, represents the life of man, the carnal man. It is the Son of Man who was tortured, crucified, and killed for teaching a truth the priests didn't understand, or want. The Son of Man was the Lamb of God.

As more and more people were listening and following His teachings, it frightened the priests who went to their king complaining. They were fearful the people would no longer adhere to their beliefs and they would lose their power over them. In their humanistic mindset, something had to be done with Jesus.

However, the Son of God with Kingdom wisdom knew what was to be. It was in the plan. He spoke to His disciples of coming to Earth to finish His Father's work. *Jesus saith unto them, My meat is to do the will of him that sent me, and to finish his work.* John 4:34 Also, *But Jesus answered them, My Father worketh hitherto, and I work.* John 5:17

When Jesus was a boy of twelve years, and after not finding Him for three days in the camp traveling home, His parents found Him in a synagogue and questioned Him. His reply was: *And he said unto them, How is it that ye sought me? wist ye not that I must be about my Father's business?* Luke 2:49 Even as a boy, Yeshua knew His place and purpose for being on earth.

Before His execution, He took His disciples to a mountaintop and spoke to them of things that would soon occur, but they didn't understand. He told them He would be leaving them soon, and they wouldn't be left alone. Afterwards, the night before they came for Him when He ate the last meal (Lord's Supper) with His twelve men in the Upper Room in Jerusalem, He explained what He was leaving with them. *And as they were eating, Jesus took bread, and blessed it, and brake it, and gave it to the disciples, and said, take, eat; this is my body. And he took the cup, and gave thanks, and gave it to them, saying, Drink ye all of it; For this is my blood of the new testament, which is shed for many for the remission of sins.* Matthew 26:26-28 Jesus gave His disciples a final instruction and a most compelling one. However, they didn't understand the symbolism of the bread and wine.

Also in the Book of Luke: *And he took bread, and gave thanks, and brake it, and gave unto them, saying, This is my body which is given for you: this do in remembrance of me. Likewise also the cup after supper, saying, This cup is the new testament in my blood, which is shed for you.* Luke 22:19-20 It was difficult for them to comprehend all the things He wanted them to know before He left His men on their own.

Jesus was explaining the representation of His body and His blood as a sacrifice (Lamb of God), for a new covenant for all mankind upon His death on the Cross. He was giving Himself that we may always be in remembrance of Him and what He has done for man.

Throughout the many generations to follow, it is something to give great homage once united with Him in Spirit. Born of His Spirit, you are intimately connected with the Son of the Most High God. Christ is your Lord.

Before Jesus surrendered Himself for the imminent crucifixion, He told them to return to the Upper Room and wait for the Comforter whom He would send. This is where Christ was with them before His death, and where He returned and spent time with them upon His resurrection before ascending to the throne.

Ten days later, for a total of fifty days from Christ's resurrection, they were all endued with supernatural Kingdom power of the Holy Spirit. The Son of God equipped His men with the same power He possessed while the Son of Man. They were now prepared to continue His ministry of the Kingdom.

Upon the Son of Man's last breath on the Cross, the veil which separated God and man was ripped in two removing the wall (sin) that kept man from God. The Son of Man died as a human person in your place on the Cross and bore your iniquities that you may become a child in the Kingdom of Heaven. The only way to your Most High God, your Almighty King, your Father is through the means that God provided and that is the *Word* becoming the Son of God, the Son of Man, the second person of the Trinity of God.

Second and presently, when the Son of God returned to the throne, what did He give to man? Notice the difference in the persons of the Son of God and Son of Man. Son of Man _did_ for man, while Son of God _gives_ to man. We shouldn't jumble everything into one concept of Christ's work. Though we know of so much He did while on Earth, there is even greater that He gives to each person who trust Him. Your humble faith, equivalent to a minuscule mustard seed, is all He is asking of you. On this minimal faith, He will provide for you. So what does the Son of God give to the newborn child of the Father?

The Son of God gives you His Spirit, His righteousness, His holiness, His authority, and supernatural Kingdom power. He gives you grace and truth. His grace is forever flowing into your life. *And of His fullness we have all received, and grace for grace. For the law was given through Moses, but grace and truth came through*

Jesus Christ. John 1:16-17 It is His grace that supplies for all your needs.

You were born self-righteous; however, in your birth of Christ's Spirit, you inherit His righteousness. You are as He is, righteous. *Herein is our love made perfect, that we may have boldness in the day of judgment: because as he is, so are we in this world.* 1 John 4:17

As Christ is seated at the right hand of the Father to whom the Father has given all things both in Heaven and on Earth; we are as He is right now. Christ gives you His authority to ask of Him and He will answer. *If ye shall ask any thing in my name, I will do it.* Romans 14:14

Could there be anything more gracious than this? Yes, even with all that the Son of God has done and given to man, there is also the gift of heavenly spiritual power. Amazing! Just when you thought you couldn't handle anymore graciousness and goodness in your life, He gives you even more…His power!

Absolutely nothing has been withheld from the child of God, because it was all meant for you in the very beginning of God's creation. It has and will remain… *all about you.* The summation is this: the Son of God gave of Himself not only as a sacrifice on the Cross, but now in the Kingdom continues to give of Himself in position, authority, and power to all who believe in Him through trust and faith.

The next obvious thought is how do you release all that the Son of God has given to you? The answer may surprise you. Mindful of the difference between a carnal and spirit life, and maintaining wisdom in God's Word with trust and faith, it is simply a matter of praise. That's correct. The answer is to praise the Son before the Father. Acknowledge all that the Son of God _did_ and *gives* to make it possible for you, a sinner destined for death, to be redeemed. Praising the Son to the Father pleases God. As He calls Christ His beloved Son, so then does He claim you as His beloved child, for in His Son, the Father sees you.

As a child of the Father, if you could grasp and hold to this knowledge, your life would be so different than what you may be enduring in your daily circumstances. Christ's authority releases the power of the Holy Spirit into your life. How else do you expect to receive a healing, or miracle if you haven't first acknowledged the principle that as Christ is in the Kingdom of Heaven, and He is in you in Spirit, so are you with Him in the Kingdom in spirit?

Born in Him, you are now where He is, and He is with you wherever you may be. Birthed with His Spirit and on His holy Name, you have His authority to ask of Him and receive. His last words as the Son of Man were: *It is finished.* Therefore, *I have glorified thee on the earth: I have finished the work which thou gavest me to do. John 17:4* Everything the Son of God and the Son of Man has accomplished is so you can be a child of the Most High God.

10

Joint Heirs in the Kingdom

The Son of God died on the Cross, arose from the dead three days later, and remained for a short period of forty days before ascending to the Kingdom to be seated on the throne. As He sits beside the Father of Creation, Christ has full jurisdiction over all things pertaining to the Kingdom of Heaven and the Kingdom of Earth.

God has bequeathed all to His Son, and His Son has given you co-ownership, a joint-heir in the Kingdom. *In whom also we have obtained an inheritance, being predestined according to the purpose of him who worketh all things after the counsel of his will.* Ephesians 1:11 What the Son owns, He shares with the children of the Father. Why? Because it was meant for you.

Christ paid the ransom, the price, that you may be reconciled to the Father in the Kingdom, forever. He came to Earth for you. Today, He is still giving to you. He gives you His authority to call upon Him for whatever you may need. He says: *ask Me and I will do it.* You have Kingdom privileges that begin the day you are born in spirit. The privileges of being a child of the Father aren't reserved for a future time such as the one-thousand year reign of Christ in the Millennium, or living in our eternal home in the New Jerusalem.

Once a joint-heir in Christ, the privileges begin. As you learn to live a spirit life with joint-ownership, you will discover that you need the heavenly provisions for your earthen life. He has made them available to you because you are no longer dependent on the worldly things, but rather the things of the spiritual Kingdom. The Father takes care of His children, just as the prodigal son is welcomed home by the father.

All gifts from the Father are spirit, and therefore, can only be accessed by your spirit through the Son's Spirit and rendered by the Holy Spirit. Think about this for a moment. God has all this wealth within His Kingdom; however, not for Himself but gave it to His Son. The Son possesses all the Kingdom treasures, but not for Himself, for they are meant for you. You have equal ownership of what Jesus' owns which is everything! *And if children, then heirs; heirs of God, and joint-heirs with Christ; if so be that we suffer with him, that we may be also glorified together.* Romans 8:17 Stop and consider how awesome this is and what it means!

We think we understand what the Father and the Son have done, but in reality, we haven't a clue of the magnificence of our Most High God. There is so much more to the love of the Father and the Son for the lost sinful children than our minds can conceive. This should give you insight in understanding God's plan, and why it was necessary for the *Word* to leave the Kingdom and finish God's work.

For four-thousand years God dealt with the people, personally. God, in His deity as Jesus and the Holy Spirit, was *among* the people, but not *in* them. Therefore, God selected specific individuals that He communicated with to carry forth His work on Earth until the time the *Word* became flesh to continue it. We witness this in Noah, Abraham, Sarah, Moses, Joshua, Solomon, David, Issac, Jacob, and there was Mary and Joseph to be the parents of Jesus, to name a few. Prophets penned the spoken words of God written for man, and Christ, the new mediator fulfilled the written word of God.

For the duration of time you have on Earth, before Christ returns a second and final time to put an end to Lucifer, you have access to the Kingdom through the Son. As long as you are focused on Him with trust shown by your faith, you may apply His authority to circumvent circumstances and events in your earthen life. It comes down to living self-righteous or righteous, being dependent on one's self, or trust in what the Son of God did for you.

This was a major problem for the Israelites, and as we have learned through history, they failed at receiving the promises of God. They wanted God to be their provider, but they didn't want to follow His statutes. They never understood the love He had for them. God never forsook them no matter how bad their behavior, but it didn't get them the riches He so desired to give to them, either.

It isn't a matter of waiting for the Son to return that you may be with Him, for He has made it possible to be with Him now, this very moment in time. He is bringing the Kingdom of Heaven down to you by way of Himself and the means of the Holy Spirit. This is truly beyond amazing, and if not careful, you can miss all the blessings just like the Israelites. It was all there before them, but they didn't accept their heavenly King.

As a co-heir in Christ and as He is in the Kingdom of Heaven, you may ask of Him and He will answer. *And whatsoever ye shall ask in my name, that will I do, that the Father may be glorified in the Son. If ye ask any thing in my name, I will do it.* John 14:13-14. This is very straightforward; however, the Son will give according to our trust in Him. You may think this is a conditional arrangement, but it isn't. Born into the Spirit realm you should be living focused on the Kingdom precepts and not worldly.

What did Jesus mean when He spoke to His disciples using the symbolism of bread as His body and said: T*his is my body given to you?* Christ is the *Bread of Life,* an eternal life, but also a life of wellness and well-being meant for today. He broke the bread to signify His body will be broken, so that your body may be healed.

As His body was beaten and literally destroyed beyond recognition, it was that you may receive heal-ing. The stripes He bore were for your health. *Who his own self bare our sins in his own body on the tree, that we, being dead to sins, should live unto righteous-ness: by whose stripes ye were healed.* 1 Peter 2:24 All the torture He endured is done specifically that you may be healed of any infirmities. In short, the destruction of His body was symbolic for the healing of yours.

His blood is shed that your blood may be sanctified, purified of sin. *My blood is shed for many for the re-mission of sins.* He shed His blood so that you would not be punished for your iniquities. It takes on a whole new meaning to say He took our place on the Cross, for literally, He freed us from the bondage of sin and the curse of disease and death.

It is extremely vital to see the relevance of what Jesus was explaining before His death. When you accept your spirit birth in Christ, you are truly born a new person. Sin, curses, and death no longer have a stronghold on you. They were destroyed in Christ for you on the Cross, forever.

Today, you should remember the last instructions given by Jesus, not only to His disciples, but to you also. He has told you that if you need a healing then ask according to His broken body. If you need forgiveness of sin, ask according to His blood shed for sin.

In understanding the communion spoken at the last meal with His disciples and applying it in your life, you will find yourself humbled by His response. So much is readily accessible to you and for you. Jesus said: *Freely, I give to you,* so the lack of receiving rests on you. *Now we have received, not the spirit of the world, but the spirit which is of God; that we might know the things that are freely given to us of God.* 1 Corinthians 2:12

All that the Son of Man <u>did</u> and the Son of God <u>gave</u> during His ministry while in the Kingdom of Earth is a cumulation at the Cross. The Father's work is finished, so that man may have a new beginning, an eternal life, that begins in Christ in the Kingdom. *He that spared not his own Son, but delivered him up for us all, how shall he not with him also freely give us all things?* Romans 8:32 The resources within the Kingdom of Heaven are available to you, a child born of God's Son, because the Son has made you a joint-heir in ownership of all the treasures within His Kingdom.

11

Power of the Spirit

C hrist gives you His *authority* to call upon heavenly resources, and it is provided to you through the Holy Spirit. God gives you His *power* through the third person of the trinity. Therefore, God as the Holy Spirit is always presenting His supernatural power into your earthen life.

It can never be said enough how important it is to understand how God planned and set forth His Kingdom, whereby His Son holds ownership. Christ shares His ownership by allowing you to become a joint-heir, an inheritance of all things that belong to Him. The Holy Spirit is the administrator of your inheritance. Just like a Last Will and Testament, or a trust fund that someone manages the distribution.

This is why when you pray, you do so on the authority given in Christ, and it is the Holy Spirit that intercedes for you as your advocate. Grasping this knowledge of how God, Elohim (Hebrew), established His Kingdom makes all the heavenly treasures available to you.

The Holy Spirit has many responsibilities to protect, provide, and teach you. He is your spokesperson within the Kingdom and knows better how to present your prayers to the Father. *Likewise the Spirit also helpeth our infirmities: for we know not what we should pray for as we ought: but the Spirit itself maketh intercession for us with groanings which cannot be uttered.* Romans 8:26

The Holy Spirit is also known as the Spirit of Truth. *Howbeit when he, the Spirit of truth, is come, he will guide you into all truth: for he shall not speak of himself; but whatsoever he shall hear, that shall he speak: and he will shew you things to come.* John 16:13 We are completely dependent upon the Spirit of Truth to teach us all matters of the Kingdom of Heaven. This is possible because we have Him within us. *Know ye not that ye are the temple of God, and that the Spirit of God dwelleth in you?* 1 Corinthians 3:16

However, just because someone receives the gift of the Holy Spirit does not mean that the Holy Spirit is actively present in their life. You have to quicken or awaken the Spirit through prayer, and then learn from Him, listen to Him, and be guided by His Kingdom wisdom. *But if the Spirit of him that raised up Jesus from the dead dwell in you, he that raised up Christ from the dead shall also quicken your mortal bodies by his Spirit that dwelleth in you.* Romans 8:11 For example, you may own a house with a swimming pool; however, if you don't swim in the water, you haven't accessed the pool. You have a pool but you don't receive any pleasure from swimming in it.

In the Old Testament era, the Holy Spirit came upon someone for God's purpose and then left. The Spirit did His work (remember, He is the power of God) and left the person. The only person that the Holy Spirit came upon and remained was Jesus. It was Christ who then gave the Holy Spirit to His disciples after He ascended to the throne.

In receiving the Holy Spirit, He lives in your heart and your physical body becomes His home. *What? know ye not that your body is the temple of the Holy Ghost which is in you, which ye have of God, and ye are not your own?* 1 Corinthians 6:19 As we have established, there are two kingdoms and principles (laws) for each. Those born of the spirit are governed by spirit laws because of the Holy Spirit.

The Holy Spirit has an encompassing role as your tutor of the Kingdom precepts, and also your protector and provider. God said He would write His laws in our heart and we would be a people to Him and He a God to us. This law that is written in your heart, the *Fruits of the Spirit,* is for the spirit person born of Christ. They are Kingdom precepts given to you to live as a spirit person.

Jesus explains the Holy Spirit to His disciples: *I have yet many things to say unto you, but ye cannot bear them now: Howbeit when he, the Spirit of truth, is come, he will guide you into all truth: for he shall not speak of himself: but whatsoever he shall hear, that shall he speak: and he will shew you things to come. He shall glorify me: for he shall receive of mine, and shall shew it unto you. All things that the Father hath are mine: therefore, said I, that he shall take of mine, and shall shew it unto you.* John 16:12-15 Your spiritual growth is through the Holy Spirit, and He is always with you.

Jesus sent the Comforter to be with His disciples as He could no longer be among them in person. *And I will pray the Father, and he shall give you another Comforter, that he may abide with you forever; Even the*

Spirit of truth; whom the world cannot receive, because it seeth him not, neither knoweth him: but ye know him; for he dwelleth with you, and shall be in you. John 14:16-17 Notice, He says that the Spirit of God will dwell <u>with</u> you and <u>in</u> you.

Many doctrines teach the giving of the Holy Spirit at Pentecost was merely for the disciples and not for us today. This is a great deception and keeps you from the knowledge and power you have at your disposal. God has a plan to give of Himself as the Son, and also as the Holy Spirit. He is giving you Kingdom power, so why wouldn't you want to access it? It's a gift. The answer is that many do not know they have such a gift.

Unfortunately, those who either teach this false doctrine, or do not speak of the Holy Spirit to their congregation, do so from ignorance; a lack of know-ledge and wisdom of the purpose of the Holy Spirit. This is merely another tactic of Satan to lead man astray from receiving God's power, for if you possess super-natural power, Lucifer has no stronghold over you.

What Christ gave to His disciples, He gives to you. It did not begin and end in one room for these men, solely; for if it did, you would have no promises forth-coming from the Father. There could be no blessings, nor gifts which include healing and miracles. Why? Because they are given through the Holy Spirit. Though it begins with His chosen men, the Comforter is given as a gift to all children upon their spirit birth into the King-dom of Heaven. *At that day ye shall know that I am in my Father, and ye in me, and I in you.* John 14:20

We refer to Pentecost as the beginning of the new Church Age; however, Pentecost which means fifty, re-presents the exact day that the Holy Ghost appeared before the one-hundred and twenty people in the Upper Room at Mount Zion in Jerusalem. It was on the fiftieth day, exactly ten days after Christ ascended to the Kingdom. Notice that upon Christ's resurrection from the dead, He spent forty days with His disciples, ascended to the throne and ten days later sent the Holy Spirit to them.

There are two *Day of Pentecost* represented in the Old and New Testaments. The first was at Mount Sinai when God gave the law, and the second at Mount Zion when Christ gave the Holy Spirit. In the giving of the Commandments, three-thousand people died because they did not believe. When Christ gave the Holy Spirit, three-thousand people lived because they believed. At Mount Sinai, they did not want to worship God and at Mount Zion, they worshipped Christ as their Lord.

In the first Day of Pentecost at Mount Sinai, God instructed Moses to bring the people up to Him in three days. Then Moses spent forty days with God. When Moses returned to the people with the Ten Command-ments, the law written on tablets of stone, the people had already made an image to worship. Moses, being angry with the people, gathered the Levites who believed in God, and killed the remaining as sinners having not accepted God as their King. Three thousand people died seven days later on the fiftieth day.

At the second Day of Pentecost at Mount Zion, Jesus having given the Holy Spirit to first His disciples and then the remaining people in the Upper Room caused a gathering of outsiders to witness the outpouring of the Spirit. On this day, three-thousand people believed and accepted the Messiah. The correlation between the two Pentecostal Days, God and Christ, is exact. The Jews celebrate Pentecost fifty days past the Feast of Passover which is Christ's death.

Once the disciples were endued with the Holy Spirit, they left the city of Jerusalem and began teaching all things taught to them by Jesus. Eventually, they were treated no differently than Christ; for again, the priests declared a false doctrine was being taught among the people, and they were martyred for such. History repeats itself.

However, the words spoken carried throughout many and as time progressed, it spun an avalanche of variation of the teachings of the Messiah, properly known as the Gospel of Christ. Today, there are more than thirty-four thousand Christian denominations regarding the Word of God. The mere thought seems hypocritical of someone so sacred.

The precepts for the spirit person comes through the Spirit of God under the covenant of Christ. The difference is the old law is for carnal man, while the new testament is for the spirit person. Because the Holy Spirit lives in your heart, these principles, *Fruits of the Spirit,* are given by the Spirit to guide your spirit person. *But the fruit of the Spirit is love, joy, peace, long-suffering, gentleness, goodness, faith, meekness, temperance: against such there is no law.* Galatians 5:22-23 He sets forth His guidelines for your behavior. This is meant to teach you how to live as a spirit person and that your demeanor changes from the worldly to the spiritual.

As the Holy Spirit is God; God is love, the off-spring should reflect love. Be gentle of heart with a spirit of love, joy, peace, goodness, gentleness, and with temperance in attitude and behavior.

As you gain wisdom and knowledge of your heavenly Father, His Son, and the Kingdom of Heaven, the Holy Spirit provides nine wonderful gifts. It is these gifts that the storehouse of treasures within the Kingdom become available to you. In the gifts, you will notice that they are all encompassing for man's life. *But the manifestation of the Spirit is given to each one for the profit withal. For to one is given the* **word of wisdom***; to another the* **word of knowledge** *by the same Spirit; To another* **faith** *by the same Spirit; to another gifts of* **healing** *by the same Spirit; To another the* **working of miracles***, to another* **prophecy***; to another* **discerning of spirits***; to another* **divers kinds of tongues***; to another the* **interpretation of tongues***. But all these worketh that one and the selfsame Spirit, dividing to every man severally as he will.* 1 Corinthians 12:7-11

What does this mean, exactly? First, these gifts belong to the Holy Spirit. We do not possess them, He does. Secondly, though you have all nine gifts available because you have the Holy Spirit, they may not all be applicable at the same time. Or, He may choose to give you more than one gift depending on the circumstance. It is by His discretion, not yours. However, His gifts are forthcoming for you.

Therefore, no one should be claiming to have the gift of healing, or the gift of prophecy, or the gift of performing miracles, and so forth, because they don't. You do not own the gift to apply at your will anywhere, anytime, for anyone, or for any reason that you deem necessary. Why? Because this is supernatural power and with your carnal soulful nature, you can easily misuse this power. And, if not careful, having such supreme power can make a person prideful. God's Kingdom power will not be handed over to man who still has the ability to be corrupted.

As you express a gift for any given situation, it is meant for that purpose only until perhaps another incident occurs that it may be required again. It is not the Holy Spirit withholding His gifts, but rather remaining in charge of them, so they are not misused. They are meant for you and are available to you, and all you have to do is ask and the Holy Spirit will discern for intervention. You may pray and ask of yourself, or others.

There probably is no other period in time that God's power is needed than today with so much disharmony and disease in people's lives. It seems everyone is touched by the forces of living in a corrupt world, and perhaps even more so, our children bare the afflictions of curses passed down through generations. To break this cycle requires an opposing supernatural power.

Satan may cause the damage, but God's power can deflect it, repair, and renew in the aftermath. More importantly, maintaining strength in God's Might, His presence and power, prevents Satan's attacks in the first place. Your only resource is the Holy Spirit. Why would you not live every single day in knowledge of His presence, depending on Him to protect you and your loved ones?

Miracles and healing are needed on a regular basis, and if you are without the Holy Spirit's presence in your life, then you will remain without a healing, or a miracle because there is only One person and His way to receive. God places Himself as the Holy Spirit within you, so that you have His supernatural power, provision, and protection.

Once you realize that these nine gifts are for every need or challenge you may face in this lifetime, it behooves you to appreciate the Holy Spirit and be dependent upon Him, continuously. Learn to rely on Him, for He will never disappoint you. After all, He is God.

12

Language of Love

God is Love and He is Spirit; therefore, it should make sense that His language would be one of the Spirit. So, if you want to communicate in the most intimate means possible with your heavenly Father, you do so in His native language. This is not an impossible task when you live as a spirit person.

God has a very special and intimate language that He gives to you as a gift, so that you may communicate personally with Him. Of the nine gifts of the Holy Spirit, the one that you may ask for and it remain with you always is *Speaking in Tongues*. Why this one? Because this is the gift that enables you to speak to your Father in His language, the language of the Spirit. It is the Holy Spirit who enables this language; thus, your carnal mind cannot understand what is spoken. It is not meant for this earthen world.

When you love a person, it is natural to want to share with them and one of the many ways we do this is through the giving of a gift. God is doing the same thing, giving you a very special gift of communication with Him. Of course, all things of God come to man as a gift, this is no exception. When you speak the heavenly language, you are edifying yourself. It is a language that strengthens your faith, gives you peace, and fortifies your life in the Spirit realm. You build your spirit up with the Spirit of God. It solidifies your faith with confidence in all things of the Father making you strong as a spirit person.

Of course, the Father hears your prayers and knows your life from conception to death, and knows every hair on your head; however, when you choose to pray to Him in a language He desires, it pleases Him. Another example of using your free will to be connected to the Kingdom of Heaven, purposefully re-moving yourself from the worldly influences. Speaking in tongues should be a natural daily occurrence for your sake, not the Father's. He already knows what is in your heart, which is why speaking in tongues edifies you.

The second application for speaking a spiritual language is in a congregation to edify the church, the people. *Wherefore tongues are a sign, not to them that believe, but to them that believe not: but prophesying serverth not for them that believe not, but for them which believe. 1* Corinthians 14:22 When speaking in tongues among a group, rightfully, there needs to be an *Interpretation of Tongues,* another gift presented by another person; otherwise, it is to no avail to understand. You cannot speak the language and also interpret at the same time. Why? There would be no witness to what was spoken. A person can speak in the spirit language and completely misunderstand the interpretation.

Many doctrines teach that the spirit language was for the disciples only and not for the generations thereafter. However, we know that Christ gives to each newborn believer the gift of the Holy Spirit. If you have the Holy Spirit, and He has gifts, then you also have those gifts available to you. Paul, who was not a disciple, and who once persecuted the Christians, had this to say: *I thank my God, I speak in tongues more than ye all.* 1 Corinthians 14:18

You have co-ownership with Christ, thus authority to call upon heavenly things, you have supernatural power available as shown to you in the nine gifts of the Holy Spirit, and you have a special spirit language, so that you may have communion with God, personally. It is not required to speak the spiritual language, and God will not be displeased if you prefer not to. It is a gift to accept or decline, no consequence from the provider.

However, as you may learn a foreign language such as Spanish, French, German, or Russian, why would you not want to speak the most important and influential language that is given to you as a gift? Speaking in tongues enables you to speak a spirit language that is understood in the Kingdom. One language is for this earthen world, a secular language, while the other is of the spirit.

Consciously choosing to not speak the spiritual language does not mean that your prayers will not be answered; however, you are the one who misses out on what speaking the spiritual language may give to you, your family, and perhaps others. We truly have no concept of the value of speaking the language of God, and the power behind it.

It is hard to imagine that every spirit born person isn't speaking continuously to their Father and His Son in a holy language of the Spirit. As you live spiritually within the Kingdom of Heaven, when you speak

Heaven's language you are right there conversing with the Father and the Son even though your carnal mind isn't privy to what is being said.

Until the Son of God returns and transforms you into your new heavenly body, this is the most absolute and intimate communication you can possibly have with the Father and the Son as you continue to live this earthen life.

13

Spiritual Persuasions

Living in a natural world, physically, and a spiritual world at the same time can be daunting for most. If you try to do it on your own merit, you will surely fail at the task because it takes spiritual guidance, not carnal thinking to live in both, simultaneously. Your soul will desire to remain influenced by the natural world, and unless you choose to relinquish yourself to be taught by the Spirit of Truth, you'll find yourself disconnected from the Kingdom of Heaven. They are separate kingdoms with entirely different perspectives which can never be combined. Always keep in mind that one is of God, and the other of Lucifer.

For example, you can't live in the United States and the United Kingdom at the same time. If you want to live in London, you must go there. Just like the difference in driving a vehicle in America verses in another country, the laws that govern are not the same. Though you are not presently living in the New Jerusalem, you have access to the Kingdom. *If ye were of the world, the world would love his own: but because ye are not of the world, but I have chosen you out of the world, therefore the world hateth you.* John 15:19 Choosing to live a spirit-led lifestyle creates a conflict sometimes within yourself and often with others. Satan doesn't want you to be spirit aware, but rather remain worldly conscious.

What does all this mean to you? It brings you full circle to acknowledging two kingdoms, two kings, two ways of living, and it all is dependent on how you use your free will. Many Christians believe they are following Christ, but then wonder why they aren't hearing from God. This should be a significant clue, but for many it still doesn't register that the channel to the Kingdom occurs when the Holy Spirit is an active participant in your life.

Resources from the two kingdoms are polar opposite. God gives you promises of blessings while Lucifer places curses on your life and your loved ones that carry down through family generations. Though Christ's death on the Cross removes curses, if you are not under the protection of the Spirit of God, a curse can come upon you even as a believer. It requires the hedge of protection that God places on you that protects you from demonic attacks. *For we wrestle not against flesh and blood, but against principalities, against powers, against the rulers of the darkness of this world, against spiritual wickedness in high places.* Ephesians 6:12

To better understand the necessity of being under the hedge of God's protection read Psalm 91, for our battle is not with flesh and blood but principalities of darkness. It has always been and remains a spiritual warfare taking place in an earthen environment, and we all are Satan's target. Therefore, the only means of salvation from his wiles is the protection God provides. *For though we walk in the flesh, we do not war after the flesh: (For the weapons of our warfare are not carnal, but mighty through God to the pulling down of strong holds;) Casting down imaginations, and every high thing that exalteth itself against the knowledge of God, and bringing into captivity every thought to the obedience of Christ.* 2 Corinthians 10:3-5

You must actively seek God's protection. God loves you and wants the very best for you and is not withholding His power, but you have a participating role in the relationship with your heavenly Father. You must be willing to accept what He desires to give to you. Relationships are not one-sided, it does take two individuals to make it work, and so it is true of your relationship with God. He is always supplying, but are you willing to receive?

Just as you have the hedge of protection, you must also be conscious to wear the armor of God to deflect anything that comes against you from the ruler of the darkness of this world. *Finally, my brethren, be strong in the Lord, and in the power of his might. Put on the whole armour of God, that ye may be able to stand against the wiles of the devil. For we wrestle not against flesh and blood, but against principalities, against powers, against the rulers of the darkness of this world, against spiritual wickedness in high places. Wherefore take unto you the whole armour of God, that ye may be able to withstand in the evil day, and having done all, to stand. Stand therefore, having your loins girt about with <u>truth</u>, and having on the breastplate of <u>righteousness</u>; And your feet shod with the preparation of the gospel of <u>peace</u>; Above all, taking the shield of <u>faith</u>, wherewith ye shall be able to quench all the fiery darts of the wicked. And take the helmet of <u>salvation</u>, and the <u>sword of the Spirit</u>,* *which is the word of God. Praying always with all prayer and supplication in the Spirit, and watching thereunto with all perseverance and supplication for all saints. Ephesians* 6:10-18 Notice, seven requirements to stand strong in the spiritual battle.

As long as you remain on this Earth, you must have the Father's protection, which He provides to you through the Holy Spirit. Once again, you can see the relevancy of having the presence of the Holy Spirit's supernatural power. The spiritual battle will continue to be waged until Christ returns. However, in the interim, God protects His children.

If you are dealing with an illness, a disease, disheartening situations, disharmony in your relationship with a spouse, children, or family; poverty, addictions, and so forth, whatever concerns you may have are all due to living in a corrupt world with an evil ruler who is a taskmaster keeping you broken and in bondage.

God is not putting bad things in your life to teach you a lesson, or draw you closer to Himself. Commonsense would tell you He doesn't need to do that, more so as a God of pure unadulterated love it is impossible to present hardship and harm. You don't love someone and purposefully harm them; it's an oxymoron.

Once you truly acknowledge the two kingdoms, you will understand that everything depends on your choice. For example, no one consciously chooses a disease but because you live in a corrupt world where it has become common to be sick, it is accepted. Often, people relate better with one another based on their illnesses and comparing their complaints.

Conversations can be summed into two categories: health, or lack thereof, and relationship breakdowns.

These circumstances you may find yourself dealing with are a component of living under the devise of a king who wants you to fail; however, God reaches out with His hand, figuratively speaking, and gives you a lifeline, a means of escape. This is living in the grace His Son gives to you.

Therefore, there appears to be three choices to not accepting God's protection. First, you don't believe in God; secondly, you do believe in the Father and His Son but have been disappointed and gave up on Him; or third, you are lacking in the knowledge of how to obtain Kingdom resources for a resolution. Notice how the last reflects on the second, and indirectly, on the first because of a lack of knowledge.

What is Satan keeping from you? The knowledge of God. He doesn't want you to learn about the other king, the One who is truly the Almighty King of all Creation, the One who presents all love and goodness, the One who gives you an eternal life within His Kingdom.

Lucifer wants you to be miserable, defeated, diseased, depressed, and die. Though he is clever, there is a way to be certain you are living within the Kingdom's spiritual realm. You choose to live by the *Fruits of the Spirit* with an outflowing of joy, peace, kindness, and love. You have complete trust in your relationship with the Son of God, and the Holy Spirit is your best friend. You live in grace which is renewed every day, and you speak often in the spirit language and receive much because it is the Father's good pleasure to give to you. It really is that simple

14

Blessings and Curses

Many Christians believe they understand the blessings of God. When asked about the curses of Satan, they become vague in response. To truly appreciate God's magnificent blessings, it requires an understanding of curses as well. Christ died on the Cross that you may be redeemed from the curses placed on your life which began with Adam.

Christ's blood was shed for the cancellation of sin, but His body hung on the tree, the Cross, to remove all curses. On the Cross, He destroyed the curse placed upon man's life by Lucifer and took death from the believer. In Christ, you have eternal life.

Think about this for a moment. Jesus was already shedding His blood for the remission of sin as He was being tortured. He didn't begin bleeding once placed on the Cross. Meaning, if it was just for the justification of sins, He did not need to be placed on a Cross, a tree branch, a stone, or anything else. But He was nailed to the Cross to deal with the curses. *Christ hath redeemed us from the curse of the law, being made a curse for us: for it is written, Cursed is every one that hangeth on a tree.* Galatians 3:13 By His body and His blood, our carnal body is put to death with Him; both sin and

curses are destroyed for you. He is the One true sacrificial lamb who took your place, not just to remove your
iniquities but also your infirmities; not the blood of an
animal but the blood of the Son of the Almighty King.

There cannot be full redemption without the destruction of curses. *Bless them which persecute you:
bless, and curse not.* Romans 12:14 Your sins are
forgiven and no longer recorded in the Book of Life;
however, curses can still remain in your life even though
Christ dealt with them on the Cross. This is one area
where Satan can continue to play havoc in your life.

Blessings are bountiful because of Christ. This is not
to say that everything in your life is perfect; however,
circumstances should always be on the blessed side
and not the degenerative one. *And God is able to make
all grace abound toward you; that ye, always having all
sufficiency in all things, may abound to every good
work.* 2 Corinthians 9:8

Grace is crucial to living a life of blessings as the
Father gives you sufficiency in all things, nothing lacking. *Blessed be the God and Father of our Lord Jesus
Christ, who hath blessed us with all spiritual blessings in
heavenly places in Christ.* Ephesians 1:3 Christ gives
you grace, not something to be earned, but a gift. As a
spirit person, this is your new environment, one of living
in grace and blessings.

Curses are from Satan. So how does a curse come
upon someone? First, you were born with a curse because of Adam. However, the expectant answer is as
simple as the next word that comes out of your mouth.
*Out of the same mouth proceedeth blessing and curs-
ing. My brethren, these things ought not so to be.* James
3:10 What you say brings either a blessing, or a curse to

yourself or another. Therefore, the easiest means by which a curse can be placed is by the use of words. That is why God instructs that the power is in the tongue. *Death and life are in the power of the tongue: and they that love it shall eat the fruit thereof.* Proverbs 18:21

There is much in the Scriptures to teach of the necessity to guard our speech. *And the tongue is a fire, a world of iniquity: so is the tongue among our members, that it defileth the whole body, and setteth on fire the course of nature; and it is set on fire of hell.* James 3:6 This is another subject that isn't taught through your typical doctrines. No one wants to speak about the presence of Satan and how he manipulates you to put curses on yourself and others.

Unless you are familiar with the war, you will surely lose the daily battle. *If any man among you seem to be religious, and bridleth not his tongue, but deceiveth his own heart, this man's religion is vain.* James 1:26 Each word that comes out of your mouth has power to do good or evil, to give a blessing or administer a curse. Guarding your tongue is more critical than one can imagine, for it can lift someone up, or destroy their life. People have committed suicide because of something said about them, a vicious tale.

If troubles abound and nothing seems to go right, think of words spoken directly to you, about you, even something you may have said. Somewhere in the mix you will discover the cause, thus the curse. Once you can identify the words or curse, rebuke it in the name of Yeshua, Jesus. That is the way to remove a curse. *Whoso keepeth his mouth and his tongue keepeth his soul from troubles.* Proverbs 21:23 Pray and rebuke the curse in the name of the Lord.

Hindrances can be emotional, physical, or spiritual that cause a state of *dis-ease* which over the course of time breaks down our bodies innate ability to replenish and repair; thus, the body succumbs to disease. It has been medically proven that guilt causes emotional digression, fear causes stress which becomes the forefront for many diseases, shame causes insecurity, and worshipping idols, statues, or symbols destroys the relationship with our heavenly Father.

Have knowledge of what God has established and not fall into worldly traps that prohibit your success in attaining your health and prosperity. The key is to not remain in bondage of this earthen ruler because when you do it changes your thoughts and emotions; and thus, your actions and beliefs.

We all will deal with unhappiness, sorrow, disappointment, emotional pain, and so forth for the simple reason of the environment we live in, but remember you are renewed in Christ and a child of the Almighty King. You are responsible for removing the blocks that keep you depressed and oppressed.

Some Kingdom blocks are not understanding God's nature, not understanding God's Kingdom precepts, lack of knowledge, and lack of application. Some common personal blocks are unforgiving, strife, curses, fear, pride, guilt, shame, grief, idolatry, hopelessness, thanklessness, lack of patience, lack of faith, lack of love, double-minded, ignorance, judgmental, and unbelief. All of these keep a person in bondage and most often, unbeknown. We simply are unaware of what is holding us captive and preventing our receiving God's power for restitution and resolution in life.

The mere definition of affliction denotes a matter of

distress, misery, or grief. A symbolic word more commonly misunderstood is the word, curses. Man causes many forms of afflictions upon himself, loved ones, friends, and strangers; individually, or as a society. *But let none of you suffer as a murderer, or as a thief, or as an evildoer, or as a busybody in other men's matters.* 1 Peter 4:15

The world events attest to this destruction. The cultural atmosphere has digressed into an ungodly state, and we are constantly under attack on a personal level as well as a national one. Whether we call it an affliction or a curse, someone has to initiate and inflict it.

There is a cause and effect ratio to everything in life, for it is an aspect of the balancing system. Curses have a negative affect and impact our lives, and we should be armored in God's Word to counter the attack. *Finally, my brethren, be strong in the Lord, and in the power of his might.* Ephesians 6:10 Though God is telling us how to be prepared for spiritual warfare, His instructions also apply in the natural, or physical world. God gives us the arsenal to use in any battlefield. An invaluable strategy of being prepared is understanding your opponent.

These attacks come in the spoken word and can lay a heavy assault on the recipient. We have an innate ability to bring forth afflictions by not guarding our tongue. It is human nature to be influenced by the words told to us, over us, or about us. Often we accept derogatory comments as the truth, because they are spoken by people we know and care about which we believe warrants their comments. Unless we are polished with knowledge and understand how curses wreak havoc in our lives, they go unchecked. The statements are never countered and nullified, destroying the curse before it takes root. *Let no corrupt communication proceed out of your mouth, but that which is good to the use of edifying, that it may minister grace unto the hearers.* Ephesians 4:29

When we think of a curse, the first thought may be the use of profanity, harsh verbiage, or something far more demonic. There is the individual who belts out comments whether slated in humor, or a deliberate act, to purposefully cause emotional injury to the recipient. This can be the most dangerous because often the person has grown accustomed to the assault and declines to retaliate, thus, breaking the curse. They become immune to the offense, especially if it occurs often, but the damage remains.

In reality, it sticks with them and does emotional, psychological, and eventually physiological harm. This is tampering with the spirit and soul of the person, a definite sin. Just because someone is unprepared to fight back, or block the curse, it is spiritually unlawful to place harm on another whether orally, or physically. We should not let our guard down in warfare. What appears on the surface to be a battle among ourselves, never underestimate that the underlying current is of a spiritual nature.

If you believe a curse has a stronghold on your life, or those you love, rebuke the words spoken. *But I say unto you, love your enemies, bless them that curse you do good to them that hate you, and pray for them which despitefully use you, and persecute you.* Matthew 5:44 Curses do affect your life whether you believe it, or not.

Summary

Life is a segment of scenes. If you take each section within this book and meditate on the content, it should render a picture of God's personages in the trinity as God, the Word, and the Holy Ghost (before man), and as the Father, the Son, and the Holy Spirit (after man). And as such, you will gain wisdom in the methodology of His Kingdom plan. See God as the Word, the Son of God, and the Son of Man, and His power through the Holy Spirit.

It reveals the relationship He has with people and the freedom of a free will letting you make the decisions that will govern your soul, spirit, and body. He desires for you to be His child and live in His Kingdom where He has prepared a place for you, but only if you want it, too. He will not coerce and force you into submission against your will. He is an Almighty King who loves His people, so much so, He refers to them as His children. He sent His Son to die in your place giving you a way to be reconcile to Him.

In the Kingdom of Earth, Lucifer claims you in slavery, in bondage, using his deceptive wiles and so subtly it often goes completely unchecked. This is how clever he is, so don't be fooled by the things of the world for they are fake, false, and futile. It becomes an effort to combat the diseases, disharmony, and destruction he regularly submits to you. Remain focused in faith on the Almighty King who loves you and live a spirit life enveloped in the love the Father and the Son have for you.

Throughout all the Scriptures, we see Christ. In the Old Testament era, spoken and worshiped by those who believed as a *shadow of things to come*. They glorified Him through the seven feasts each year: Passover, Unleavened Bread, First Fruits, Pentecost, Trumpets, Atonement, and Tabernacles. This continues today among the Jews, specifically those who live in the homeland of the Messiah, Jerusalem, and all of Israel. The lamb's blood shed was the representation until the true Lamb of God shed His blood for man.

In the New Testament, we learn how Jesus served the people through numerous miracles and healing. *For even the Son of man came not to be ministered unto, but to minister, and to give his life a ransom for many.* Mark 10:45 And to think all were sinners, not yet born of His Spirit. On the last night before His betrayal, Jesus washed the feet of His disciples, an example of His servitude. He fed the fisherman breakfast on the shoreline after His resurrection.

As He came to serve the people before His death, He continues even in His deity on the throne to serve you with His Spirit, giving you grace, righteousness, and holiness; cleansed, purified, and prepared for the holy Kingdom.

What has been established at Creation has been set forth for man. It was never God's intent that man should suffer with disease, disharmony, destruction, and death. Man was fashioned a spirit person to live as a child of God. But God knew that Lucifer would betray Him, and that Adam would disobey Him, and yet, He still loved

Adam. He has never stopped loving the generations of people since Adam though they were a corrupt and sinful people.

Even when the Israelites rejected Him as their King, He took care of them in the desert, and all through time we witness His everlasting love for man. Because God is the same, never changing, His love remains true, never conditional.

You are so precious to Him that He came to a corrupt sinful world to save you from death. God's plan is for you to live with Him forever; however, Satan's plan is your demise. The Almighty King of all Creation stepped down from His throne within the Kingdom of Heaven and came to the Kingdom of Earth to rescue you. However, you must want to be saved.

The Israelites didn't want what God gave them. It took forty years until the next generation, their children, were willing to accept God as their King and finally Joshua guided them into the promised land planned for their forefathers. If you do not use your free will wisely, and refuse what God is giving you, then you are lost to Him by your choice, not His. You don't have to be born of His Spirit, but the finality of your natural life is death.

It is your decision to be born into His Kingdom and receive an eternal life that begins the day you accept His Son. It doesn't start and stop with just an admission in a prayer. Rightfully, your growth in the spirit has begun setting you on a new path, for the sinful carnal you is now buried in Christ on the Cross. With the gift that Christ gives, the Holy Spirit, you have a passport into the Kingdom of Heaven. It's dependent upon you to use often, making daily trips into the Kingdom for wisdom, healing, miracles, prosperity, better relation-ships, and so forth. It is a free entrance pass giving you the authority and power that comes with it.

You are used to the regulations of the Kingdom of Earth, but you will find the Kingdom of Heaven quite different, one you are unaccustomed to, for it is in com-plete opposition to everything you know. You will need to learn how to live in this new Kingdom, how to access the storehouse of treasures, and how to utilize the dunamis power of the Spirit of God. You are a child of the Most High God, and all is yours because everything God and the Word created, and the Father and the Son did was for you.

You have a role to play in this scene and that is to receive, but you can't receive until you accept, and you can't accept until you have knowledge, and you don't get knowledge until you use your free will and make a choice to live a spirit life. Nothing will ever be more important than your decision to choose Jesus' saving grace and the Kingdom of Heaven.

Excerpts from the book

Everlasting Love, God's Greatest Gift

Names and Titles of Christ

There are over two hundred names and titles in the Bible for Jesus Christ. The specific names given to Christ, and the numerous titles He held, depicts that everything God created was about the Living Word who left His throne and dwelt among us, and to every believer, is now in us.

Throughout the generations spanning nearly six thousand years from the Book of Genesis to the final book of Revelation is a reflection of the life of Christ. We see Him as both the Son of God when He was spoken of as *a shadow of things to come* in the Old Testament to the Son of Man, His time on earth as a human being as taught in the New Testament. Soon Christ will return again for a final appearance.

ADAM: And so it is written, The first man **Adam** was made a living soul; the last **Adam** was made a quickening spirit. 1 Corinthians 15:45

ADVOCATE: My little children, these things write I unto you, that ye sin not. And if any man sin, we have an **advocate** with the Father, Jesus Christ the righteous. 1 John 2:1

ALMIGHTY: I am Alpha and Omega, the beginning and the ending, saith the Lord, which is, and which was, and which is to come, the **Almighty**. Revelation 1:8

ALPHA AND OMEGA: I am **Alpha** and **Omega**, the beginning and the ending, saith the Lord, which is, and which was, and which is to come, the Almighty. Revelation 1:8

AMEN: And unto the angel of the church of the Laodiceans write; These things saith the **Amen**, the faithful and true witness, the beginning of the creation of God. Revelation 3:14

APOSTLE OF OUR PROFESSION: Wherefore, holy brethren, partakers of the heavenly calling, consider the **Apostle** and High Priest **of our profession**, Christ Jesus. Hebrews 3:1

ARM OF THE LORD: Awake, awake, put on strength, O **arm of the Lord**; awake, as in the ancient days, in the generations of old. Art thou not it that hath cut Rahab, and wounded the dragon? Who hath believed our report? And to whom is the arm of the Lord revealed? Isaiah 53:1; and Isaiah 51: 9

AUTHOR AND FINISHER OF OUR FAITH: Looking unto Jesus **the author and finisher of our faith**; who for the joy that was set before him endured the cross, despising the shame, and is set down at the right hand of the throne of God. Hebrews 12:2

AUTHOR OF ETERNAL SALVATION: And being made

perfect, he became the **author of eternal salvation** unto all them that obey him. Hebrews 5:9

BEGINNING OF CREATION OF GOD: And unto the angel of the church of the Laodiceans write; These things saith the Amen, the faithful and true witness, the **beginning of the creation of God**. Revelation 3:14

BELOVED SON: Behold my servant, whom I have chosen; my **beloved**, in whom my soul is well pleased: I will put my spirit upon him, and he shall show judgment to the Gentiles. Matthew 12:18

BLESSED AND ONLY POTENTATE: Which in his times he shall show, who is the **blessed and only Potentate**, the King of kings, and Lord of lords. 1 Timothy 6:15

BRANCH: In that day shall the **branch** of the Lord be beautiful and glorious, and the fruit of the earth shall be excellent and comely for them that are escaped of Israel. Isaiah 4:2

BREAD OF LIFE FROM HEAVEN: Then Jesus said unto them, Verily, verily, I say unto you, Moses gave you not that **bread from heaven**; but my Father giveth you the true **bread from heaven**. John 6:32

CAPTAIN OF SALVATION: For it became him, for whom are all things, and by whom are all things, in bringing many sons unto glory, to make the **captain of their salvation** perfect through sufferings. Hebrews 2:10

CHIEF SHEPHERD: And when the **chief Shepherd** shall appear, ye shall receive a crown of glory that fadeth not away. 1 Peter 5:4

CHRIST OF GOD: He said unto them, But whom say ye that I am? Peter answering said, The **Christ of God**. Luke 9:20

CONSOLATION OF ISRAEL: And, behold, there was a man in Jerusalem, whose name was Simeon; and the same man was just and devout, waiting for the **consolation of Israel**: and the Holy Ghost was upon him. Luke 2:25

CHIEF CORNERSTONE: The stone which the builders refused is become the head stone of the corner. And are built upon the foundation of the apostles and prophets, Jesus Christ himself being the **chief corner stone**; In who all the building fitly framed together groweth unto a holy temple in the Lord. Psalm 118:22; Ephesians 2:20-21

COUNSELLOR: For unto us a child is born, unto us a son is given: and the government shall be upon his shoulder: and his name shall be called Wonderful, **Counsellor**, The Mighty God, The Everlasting Father, The Prince of Peace. Isaiah 9:6

CREATOR: All things were made by him; and without him was not any thing made that was made. Who is the image of the invisible God, the firstborn of every creature: For by him were all things **created**, that are in heaven, and that are in earth, visible and invisible, whether they be thrones, or dominions, or principalities, or powers: all things were **created** by him, and for him: and he is before all things, and by all things consist. Colossians 1:15-16; John 1:3

DAYSPRING: Through the tender mercy of our God; whereby the **dayspring** from on high hath visited us. Luke 1:78

DELIVERER: And so all Israel shall be saved: as it is written, There shall come out of Sion the **Deliverer**, and shall turn away ungodliness from Jacob. Romans 11:26

DESIRE OF THE NATIONS: And I will shake all nations, and the **desire of all nations** shall come: and I will fill this house with glory, saith the Lord of hosts. Haggai 2:7

DOOR: Then said Jesus unto them again, Verily, verily, I say unto you, I am the **door** of the sheep. John 10:7

ELECT OF GOD: Behold my servant, whom I uphold; **mine elect**, in whom my soul delighteth; I have put my spirit upon him: he shall bring forth judgment to the Gentiles. Isaiah 42:1

EVERLASTING FATHER: For unto us a child is born, unto us a son is given: and the government shall be upon his shoulder: and his name shall be called Wonderful, Counsellor, The Mighty God, The **Everlasting Father**, The Prince of Peace. Isaiah 9:6

FAITHFUL WITNESS: And from Jesus Christ, who is the **faithful witness**, and the first begotten of the dead, and the prince of the kings of the earth. Unto him that loved us, and washed us from our sins in his own blood. Revelation 1:5

FIRST AND LAST: And when I saw him, I fell at his feet as dead. And he laid his right hand upon me, saying unto me, Fear not; I am the **first and the last**. Revelation 1:17

FIRST BEGOTTEN: And from Jesus Christ, who is the faithful witness, and the **first begotten** of the dead, and the prince of the kings of the earth. Unto him that loved us, and washed us from our sins in his own blood. Revelation 1:5

FORERUNNER: Whither the **forerunner** is for us entered, even Jesus, made an high priest forever after the order of Melchisedec. Hebrews 6:20

GLORY OF THE LORD: And the **glory of the Lord** shall be revealed, and all flesh shall see it together: for the mouth of the Lord hath spoken it. Isaiah 40:5

GOD: The voice of him that crieth in the wilderness, Prepare ye the way of the Lord, make straight in the desert a highway for our **God**. Isaiah 40: 3

GOD BLESSED: Whose are the fathers, and of whom as concerning the flesh Christ came, who is over all, **God blessed** forever. Amen. Romans 9:5

GOOD SHEPHERD: I am the **good shepherd**: the **good shepherd** giveth his life for the sheep. John 10:11

GOVERNOR: And thou Bethlehem, in the land of Juda, art not the least among the princes of Juda: for out of thee shall come a **Governor**, that shall rule my people Israel. Matthew 2:6

GREAT HIGH PRIEST: Seeing then that we have a **great high priest**, that is passed into the heavens, Jesus the Son of God, let us hold fast our profession. Hebrews 4:14

HEAD OF THE CHURCH: And hath put all things under his feet, and gave him to be the **head over all things to the church**. Ephesians 1:22

HEIR OF ALL THINGS: Hath in these last days spoken unto us by his Son, whom he hath appointed **heir of all things**, by whom also he made the worlds. Hebrews 1:2

HOLY CHILD: For of a truth agains thy **holy child** Jesus, who thou hast anointed, both Herod, and Pontius Pilate, with the Gentiles, and the people of Israel, were gathered together. Acts 4:27

HOLY ONE: But ye denied the **Holy One** and the Just, and desired a murderer to be granted unto you. Acts 3:14

HOLY ONE OF GOD: Saying, Let us alone; what have we to do with thee, thou Jesus of Nazareth? Art thou come to destroy us? I know thee who thou art, the **Holy One of God**. Mark 1:24

HOLY ONE OF ISRAEL: Fear not, thou worm Jacob, and

ye men of Israel; I will help thee, saith the Lord, and thy redeemer, the **Holy One of Israel**. Isaiah 41:14

HORN OF SALVATION: And hath raised up an **horn of salvation** for us in the house of his servant David. Luke 1:69

I AM: Jesus said unto them,Verily, verily, I say unto you, Before Abraham was, **I am**. John 8:58

IMAGE OF GOD: In whom the god of this world hath blinded the minds of them which believe not, lest the light of the glorious gospel of Christ, who is the **image of God**, should shine unto them. 2 Corinthians 4:4

IMMANUEL: Therefore the Lord himself shall give you a sign; Behold, a virgin shall conceive, and bear a son, and shall call his name **Immanuel**. Isaiah 7:14

JEHOVAH: Trust ye in the Lord for ever: for in the Lord **Jehovah** is everlasting strength. Isaiah 26:4

JESUS: And she shall bring forth a son, and thou shalt call his name **Jesus** for he shall save his people from their sins. Matthew 1:21

JESUS OF NAZARETH: And the multitude said, This is **Jesus** the prophet **of Nazareth** of Galilee. Matthew 21:11

JUDGE OF ISRAEL: Now gather thyself in troops, O daughter of troops: he hath laid siege against us: they shall smite the **judge of Israel** with a rod upon the cheek. Micah 5:1

THE JUST ONE: Which of the prophets have not your fathers persecuted? And they have slain them which showed before of the coming of the **Just One**; of whom ye have been now the betrayers and murderers. Acts 7: 52

KING: Rejoice greatly, O daughter of Zion; shout, O daughter of Jerusalem: behold, thy **King** cometh unto thee: he is just, and having salvation; lowly, and riding upon an ass, and upon a colt the foal of an ass. Zechariah 9:9

KING OF THE AGES: Now unto the **King eternal**, immortal, invisible, the only wise God, be honour and glory for ever and ever. Amen. 1 Timothy 1:17

KING OF THE JEWS: Saying, Where is he that is born **King of the Jews**? For we have seen his star in the east, and are come to worship him. Matthew 2:2

KING OF KINGS: Which in his times he shall show, who is the blessed and only Potentate, the **King of kings**, and Lord of lords. 1 Timothy 6:15

KING OF SAINTS: And they sing the song of Moses the servant of God, and the song of the Lamb, saying, Great and marvelous are thy works, Lord God Almighty; just and true are thy ways, thou **King of saints**. Revelation 15:3

LAWGIVER: For the Lord is our judge, the Lord is our **lawgiver**, the Lord is our king; he will save us. Isaiah 33:22

LAMB: And all that dwell upon the earth shall worship him, whose names are not written in the book of life of the **Lamb** slain from the foundation of the world. Revelation 13:8

LAMB OF GOD: The next day John seeth Jesus coming unto him, and saith, Behold the **Lamb of God**, which taketh away the sin of the world. John 1:29

LEADER AND COMMANDER: Behold, I have given him for a witness to the people, a **leader and commander** to the people. Isaiah 55:4

THE LIFE: Jesus saith unto him, I am the way, the truth, and **the life**: no man cometh unto the Father, but by me. John 14:6

LIGHT OF THE WORLD: Then spake Jesus again unto them, saying, I am the **light of the world**: he that followeth me shall not walk in darkness, but shall have the light of life. John 8:12

LION OF THE TRIBE OF JUDAH: And one of the elders saith unto me, Weep not: behold, the **Lion of the tribe of Juda**, the Root of David, hath prevailed to open the book, and to loose the seven seals thereof. Revelation 5:5

LORD OF ALL: The word which God sent unto the

children of Israel, preaching peace by Jesus Christ: (he is **Lord of all**). Acts 10:36

LORD OF GLORY: Which none of the princes of this world knew: for had they known it, they would not have crucified the **Lord of glory**. 1 Corinthians 2:8

LORD OF LORDS: Which in his times he shall show, who is the blessed and only Potentate, the King of kings, and **Lord of lords**. 1 Timothy 6:15

LORD OF OUR RIGHTEOUSNESS: In this days Judah shall be saved, and Israel shall dwell safely: and this is his name whereby he shall be called, The **Lord our Righteousness**. Jeremiah 23:6

MAN OF SORROWS: He is despised and rejected of men; a **man of sorrows**, and acquainted with grief: and we hid as it were our faces from him; he was despised, and we esteemed him not. Isaiah 53:3

MEDIATOR: For there is one God, and one **mediator** between God and men, the man Christ Jesus. 1 Timothy 2:5

MESSENGER OF THE COVENANT: Behold, I will send my messenger, and he shall prepare the way before me: and the Lord, whom ye seek, shall suddenly come to his temple, even the **messenger of the covenant**, whom ye delight in: behold, he shall come, saith the Lord of hosts. Malachi 3:1

MESSIAH: Know therefore and understand, that from

the going forth of the commandment to restore and to build Jerusalem unto the **Messiah** the Prince shall be seven weeks, and threescore and two weeks: the street shall be built again, and the wall, even in troublous times. Daniel 9:26 He first findeth his own brother Simon, and saith unto him, We have found the **Messiah**, which is, being interpreted, the Christ. John 1:41

MIGHTY GOD: For unto us a child is born, unto us a son is given: and the government shall be upon his shoulder: and his name shall be called Wonderful, Counsellor, The **Mighty God**, The Everlasting Father, The Prince of Peace. Isaiah 9:6

MIGHTY ONE: Thou shalt also suck the milk of the Gentiles, and shalt suck the breast of kings: and thou shalt know that I the Lord am thy Saviour and thy Redeemer, the **mighty One** of Jacob. Isaiah 60:16

MORNING STAR: I Jesus have sent mine angel to testify unto you these things in the churches. I am the root and the offspring of David, and the bright and **morning star**. Revelation 22:16

NAZARENE: And he came and dwelt in a city called **Nazareth**: that it might be fulfilled which was spoken by the prophets, He shall be called a **Nazarene**. Matthew 2:23

ONLY BEGOTTEN SON: No man hath seen God at any time; the **only begotten Son**, which is in the bosom of the Father, he hath declared him. John 1:18

OUR PASSOVER: Purge out therefore the old leaven, that ye may be a new lump, as ye are unleavened. For even Christ **our passover** is sacrificed for us. 1 Corinthians 5:7

PRINCE OF LIFE: And killed the **Prince of life**, whom God hath raised from the dead; whereof we are witnesses. Acts 3:15

PRINCE OF KINGS: And from Jesus Christ, who is the faithful witness, and the first begotten of the dead, and the **prince of the kings** of the earth. Unto him that loved us, and washed us from our sins in his own blood. Revelation 1:5

PRINCE OF PEACE: For unto us a child is born, unto us a son is given: and the government shall be upon his shoulder: and his name shall be called Wonderful, Counsellor, The Mighty God, The Everlasting Father, The **Prince of Peace**. Isaiah 9:6

PROPHET: And he said unto them, What things? And they said unto him, Concerning Jesus of Nazareth, which was a **prophet** mighty in deed and word before God and all the people. For Moses truly said unto the fathers, A **prophet** shall the Lord your God raise up unto you of your brethren, like unto me; him shall ye hear in all things whatsoever he shall say unto you. Acts 3:22; Luke 24:19

REDEEMER: For I know that my **redeemer** liveth, and that he shall stand at the latter day upon the earth. Job 19:25

RESURRECTION AND LIFE: Jesus said unto her, I am the **resurrection and the life**: he that believeth in me, though he were dead, yet shall he live. John 11:25

ROCK: And did all drink the same spiritual drink: for they drank of that spiritual **Rock** that followed them: and that **Rock** was Christ. 1 Corinthians 10:4

ROOT OF DAVID: I Jesus have sent mine angel to testify unto you these things in the churches. I am the **root** and the offspring **of David**, and the bright and morning star. Revelation 22:16

ROSE OF SHARON: I am the **rose of Sharon**, and the lily of the valleys. Solomon 2:1

SAVIOUR: For unto you is born this day in the city of David a **Saviour**, which is Christ the Lord. Luke 2:1

SEED OF WOMAN: And I will put enmity between thee and the woman, and between thy seed and **her seed**; it shall bruise thy head, and thou shalt bruise his heel. Genesis 3:15

SHEPHERD AND BISHOP OF SOULS: For ye were as sheep going astray; but are now returned unto the **Shepherd and Bishop of your souls**. 1 Peter 2:25

SHILOH: The scepter shall not depart from Judah, nor a lawgiver from between his feet, until **Shiloh** come; and unto him shall the gathering of the people be. Genesis 49:10

SON OF THE BLESSED: But he held his peace, and answered nothing. Again the high priest asked him, and said unto him, Art thou the Christ, the **Son of the Blessed**? Mark 14:61

SON OF DAVID: The book of the generation of Jesus Christ, the **son of David**, the son of Abraham. Matthew 1:1

SON OF GOD: And was there until the death of Herod: that it might be fulfilled which was spoken of the Lord by prophet, saying, Out of Egypt have I called **my son**. Matthew 2:15

SON OF THE HIGHEST: He shall be great, and shall be called the **Son of the Highest**: and the Lord God shall give unto him the throne of his father David. Luke 1:32

SUN OF RIGHTEOUSNESS: But unto you that fear my name shall the **Sun of Righteousness** arise with healing in his wings; and ye shall go forth, and grow up as calves of the stall. Malachi 4:2

TRUE LIGHT: That was the **true Light**, which lighteth every man that cometh into the world. John 1:9

TRUE VINE: I am the **true vine**, and my Father is the husbandman. John 15:1

TRUTH: And the Word was made flesh, and dwelt among us, (and we beheld his glory, the glory as of the only begotten of the Father,) full of grace and **truth**. John 1:14

WITNESS: Behold, I have given him for a **witness** to the people, a leader and commander to the people. Isaiah 55:4

WORD: In the beginning was the **Word**, and the **Word** was with God, and the **Word** was God. John 1:1

WORD OF GOD: And he was clothed with a vesture dipped in blood: and his name is called The **Word of God**. Revelation 19:13

The Trinity in Christ

In understanding the Trinity of God, we witness the relevance of God's creation and all God fashioned at the foundation was defined in His Son, Jesus, the Word. *For by him were all things created, that are in heaven, and that are in earth, visible and invisible, whether they be thrones, or dominions, or principalities, or powers: all things were created by him, and for him: And he is before all things, and by him all things consist.* Colossians 1:16-17 We can see God's work manifested through the nature, position, and works of His Son.

The Nature of Christ

CHIEF CORNERSTONE – Jesus is the cornerstone of the building which is His church. He cements together Jew and Gentile, male and female; all saints from all ages and places into one structure built on faith in Him which is shared by all. *And are built upon the foundation of the apostles and prophets, Jesus Christ himself being the* **chief corner stone***; In whom all the building fitly framed together groweth unto an holy temple in the Lord.* Ephesians 2:20-21

FIRSTBORN OVER ALL CREATION - Not the first thing God created, but that Christ occupies the rank and preeminence of the firstborn over all things, that He sustains the most exalted rank in the universe. He is preeminent above all others; He is at the head of all things. *Who is the image of the invisible God, the* **firstborn** *of every creature: For by him were all things created, that are in heaven, and that are in earth, visible and invisible, whether they be thrones, or dominions, or principalities, or powers: all things were created by him, and for him: and he is before all things, and by all things consist.* Colossians 1:15-16

HEAD OF THE CHURCH - Jesus Christ, not a king or a pope, is the only supreme, sovereign ruler of the Church. *And hath put all things under his feet, and gave him to be the head over all things to the church, Which is his body, the fulness of him that filleth all in all.* Also, *For the husband is the head of the wife, even as Christ is the* **head of the church**: *and he is the saviour of the body.* Ephesians 1:22-23; 5:23

HOLY ONE - Christ is holy, both in His divine and human nature, and the fountain of holiness to His people. By His death, we are made holy and pure before God. *But ye denied the* **Holy One** *and the Just, and desired a murderer to be granted unto you; And killed the Prince of life, whom God hath raised from the dead; whereof we are witnesses.* Also, *For thou will not leave my soul in hell; neither wilt thou suffer thine* **Holy One** *to see corruption.* Acts 3:14; Psalm 16:10

JUDGE - The Lord Jesus was appointed by God to judge the world and to dispense the rewards of eternity. *And he commanded us to preach unto the people, and to testify that it is he which was ordained of God to be the* **Judge** *of quick and dead.* Also, Henceforth *there is laid up for me a crown of righteousness, which the Lord, the righteous* **Judge**, *shall give me at that day: and not to me only, but unto all them also that love his appearing.* And, *And hath given him authority to execute judgment also, because he is the Son of man; For the Lord is our* **Judge**, *the Lord is our lawgiver, the Lord is our king; he will save us.* Acts 10:42; 2 Timothy 4:8; John 5:27

KING OF KINGS AND LORD OF LORDS - Jesus is King and has dominion over all authority on the earth, over all kings and rulers of this world. *Which in his times he shall show, who is the blessed and only Potentate, the* **King of kings, and Lord of lords**. Also, *And he hath on his vesture and on his thigh a name written,* **King of kings, and Lord of Lords**. 1 Timothy 6:15; Revelation 19:16

LIGHT OF THE WORLD - Jesus came into a world darkened by sin and shed the light of life and truth through His work and His words. *Then spake Jesus unto them, saying, I am the* **light of the world**: *he that followeth me shall not walk in darkness, but shall have the light of life.* John 8:12

PRINCE OF PEACE - Jesus came to bring peace to the world and remove the sin that came between God and man. He died to reconcile sinners to a holy God. *For unto us a child is born, unto us a son is given: and the government shall be upon his shoulder: and his name shall be called Wonderful, Counsellor, The mighty God,*

*The everlasting Father, **The Prince of Peace**. Isaiah 9:6*

SON OF GOD – Jesus is the only begotten of the Father and, therefore, is the Son of God. This is revealed throughout the New Testament. *And the angel answered and said unto her, The Holy Ghost shall come upon thee, and the power of the Highest shall over-shadow thee: therefore also that holy thing shall be born of thee shall be called the **Son of God**. Also, For God so loved the world, that he gave his only begotten Son, that whosoever believeth in him should not perish, but have everlasting life; And we know that the **Son of God** is come, and hath given us an understanding, that we may know him that is true, and we are in him that is true, even in his Son Jesus Christ. This is the true God, and eternal life, Nathanael answered and saith unto him, Rabbi, thou art the **Son of God**; thou art the King of Israel. And, And the Word was made flesh, and dwelt among us, (and we beheld his glory, the glory as of the only begotten of the Father), full of grace and truth.* Luke 1:35; John 3:16; John 1:14; 1:49; 1 John 5:20

SON OF MAN – Son of God and Son of Man are personages of Jesus Christ. Son of Man affirms the humanity of Christ in His divinity as the Son of God. It depicts His all encompassing authority of man. *For the Father hath life in himself; so hath he given to the Son to have life in himself; And hath given him authority to execute judgment also, because he is the **Son of man**.* John 5:27

WORD – The Word is the second person, Jesus Christ, of the trinity of God, who spoke all things out of nothing in the first creation, who was in the beginning with God the Father, and was God, and by whom all things were created. *In the beginning was the **Word**, and the **Word** was with God, and the **Word** was God.* Also, *For there are three that bear record in heaven, the Father, the **Word**, and the Holy Ghost: and these three are one. And there are three that bear witness in earth, the Spirit, and the water, and the blood: and these three agree in one.* John 1:1; 1 John 5:7-8

WORD OF GOD - This is the name given to Christ that is unknown to all but Himself. It denotes the mystery of His divine person. *His eyes were as a flame of fire, and on his head were many crowns; and he had a name written, that no man knew, but he himself. And he was clothed with a vesture dipped in blood: and his name is called The **Word of God**.* Revelation 19:12-13

WORD OF LIFE - Jesus not only spoke words that would give us eternal life, but He is the very words of life. *That which was from the beginning, which we have heard, which we have seen with our eyes, which we have looked upon, and our hands have handled, of the **Word of life**.* 1 John 1:1

Christ's Position in the Trinity

ALPHA AND OMEGA - We know God and Christ to be as One in the trinity. God is Christ and Jesus is God. As One deity, they are the Alpha and Omega of all creation. *I am the **Alpha and Omega**, the beginning and the end, saith the Lord, which is, and which was, and* which is to come, the Almighty. Also, *I am the* **Alpha and Omega**, *the beginning and the end, the first and the last. And, And he said unto me, It is done. I am* **Alpha and Omega**, *the beginning and the end, I will give unto him that is athirst of the fountain of the water of life freely.* Revelation 1:8; 22:13; 21:6

EMMANUEL – God came to earth in the second person of the trinity, Christ, born of flesh to live among His people. *Behold, a virgin shall be with child, and shall bring forth a son, and they shall call his name* **Emmanuel**, *which being interpreted is, God with us.* Matthew 1:23

I AM – We can see the deity of God and Christ as One. Both God and Jesus declare to the people their omnipresence. *And God said unto Moses,* **I am** *that* **I am***: and he said, Thus shalt thou say unto the children of Israel,* **I am** *hath sent me unto you.* Also, *Jesus said unto them, Verily, verily, I say unto you, Before Abraham was,* **I am**. Exodus 3:14; John 8:58

LORD OF ALL – Jesus is King over all things. The Father gave all creation to His Son. *The word which God sent unto the children of Israel, preaching peace by Jesus Christ (he is* **Lord of all***:) That word, I say, ye know, which was published throughout all Judaea, and began from Galilee after the baptism which John preached; How God anointed Jesus of Nazareth with the Holy Ghost and with power: who went about doing good, and healing all that were oppressed of the devil; for God was with him.* Acts 10:36-38

TRUE GOD – God and Jesus are One Divinity, for God

came to earth as Christ, and God is Jesus. In the personage of Christ, God reveals a part of His nature. *And we know that the Son of God is come, and hath given us an understanding, that we may know him that is true, and we are in him that is true, even in his Son Jesus Christ. This is the* **true God**, *and eternal life.* 1 John 5:20

Christ's Work on Earth

AUTHOR AND PERFECTER OF OUR FAITH - Eternal life is accomplished through the faith that is the gift of God, and Jesus is the founder of our faith and the finisher of it as well. From first to last, He is the source and sustainer of the faith that saves us. *Looking unto Jesus* **the author and finisher of our faith**; *who for the joy that was set before him endured the cross, despising the shame, and is set down at the right hand of the throne of God.* Also, *For by grace are ye saved through faith; and that not of yourselves: it is the gift of God. Not of works, lest any man should boast.* Hebrews 12:2; Ephesians 2:8-9

BREAD OF LIFE - Just as bread sustains life in the physical sense, Jesus is the bread that gives and sustains eternal life. God provided manna in the wilderness to feed His people, and He provided Jesus to give us eternal life through His body, broken for us. *And Jesus said unto them, I am the* **bread of life,** *he that cometh to me shall never hunger, and he that believeth on me shall never thirst.* Also, *I am the* **bread**

of life. Your fathers did eat manna in the wilderness, and are dead. This is the bread which cometh down from heaven, that a man may eat thereof, and not die. I am the living bread which came down from heaven: if any man eat of this bread, he shall live for ever: and the bread that I will give is my flesh, which I will give for the life of the world. John 6:35; 6:48-51

BRIDEGROOM - Christ is the Bridegroom and the faithful saints are His bride. We are bound to Jesus in a covenant of grace that sets us apart as we wait for our bridegroom to come for us. *And Jesus said unto them, Can the children of the bride chamber mourn, as long as the* **bridegroom** *is with them? But the days will come, when the* **bridegroom** *shall be taken from them, and then shall they fast. Also, Then shall the kingdom of heaven be likened unto ten virgins, which took their lamps, and went to meet the* **bridegroom;** *And at midnight there was a cry made, Behold, the* **bridegroom** *cometh; go ye out to meet him.* Matthew 9:15; 25:1; 25:6

DELIVERER - Just as the Israelites needed God to deliver them from bondage to Egypt, so Christ is our Deliverer from the bondage of sin. *And so all Israel shall be saved: as it is written, There shall come out of Sion the* **Deliverer**, *and shall turn away ungodliness from Jacob: For this is my covenant unto them, when I shall take away their sins.* Romans 11:26-27

GOOD SHEPHERD - A good shepherd is willing to risk his life to protect his sheep from predators. Jesus laid down His life for His sheep to gather us to Him in faith. He provides and protects us from worldly predators.

*I am the **good shepherd**: for the **good shepherd** giveth his life for the sheep. Also, I am the **good shepherd**, and know my sheep, and am known of mine.* John 10:11; 10:14

HIGH PRIEST - The Jewish high priest entered the temple once a year to make atonement for the sins of the people. Jesus did this once for all at the cross. *Wherefore, holy brethren, partakers of the heavenly calling, consider the Apostle and **High Priest** of our profession, Christ Jesus. Also, Seeing then that we have a great **high priest**, that is passed into the heavens, Jesus the Son of God, let us hold fast our profession. And, For verily he took not on him the nature of angels; but he took on him the seed of Abraham. Wherefore in all things it behoved him to be made like unto his brethren, that he might be a merciful and faithful in things pertaining to God, to make a reconciliation for the sins of the people; Whither the forerunner is for us entered, even Jesus, made an **high priest** for ever after the order of Melchisedec.* Hebrews 3:1; 4:14; 2:16-17; 6:20

LAMB OF GOD - God's law called for the sacrifice of a spotless, unblemished lamb as an atonement for sin. Jesus became that lamb showing His patience in His sufferings and His readiness to die for His own. *The next day John seeth Jesus coming unto him, and saith, Behold the **Lamb of God**, which taketh away the sin of the world. Also, And looking upon Jesus as he walked, he saith, Behold the **Lamb of God**.* John 1:29; 1:36

MEDIATOR - A mediator is one who goes between two parties to reconcile them. Christ is the one and only mediator who reconciles man to God. *For there is one God, and one **mediator** between God and men, the man Christ Jesus; Who gave himself a ransom for all to be testified in due time.* Also, *But now hath he obtained a more excellent ministry, by how much also he is the **mediator** of a better covenant, which was established upon better promises; For this cause he is the **mediator** of the new testament, that by means of death, for the redemption of the transgressions that were under the first testament, they which are called might receive the promises of eternal inheritance; And to Jesus the **mediator** of the new covenant, and to the blood of sprinkling, that speaketh better things than that of Abel.* 1 Timothy 2:5-6; Hebrews 8:8; 9:15; 12:24

ROCK - As life-giving water flowed from the rock Moses struck in the wilderness, Jesus is the Rock from which flows the living waters of eternal life. He is the Rock upon whom we build our spiritual house. *And did all drink the same spiritual drink: for they drank of that spiritual **Rock** that followed them: and that **Rock** is Christ.* 1 Corinthians 10:4

RESURRECTION AND LIFE - Jesus is the means to resurrect sinners to eternal life, just as He was resurrected from the grave. Our sin is buried with Him nailed at the cross, and we are resurrected to walk in newness of life. *Jesus said unto her, I am the **resurrection, and the life**: he that believeth in me, though he were dead, yet shall he live.* Also, *And with great power gave the apostles witness of the resurrection of the Lord Jesus: and great grace was upon them all.* John 11:25; Acts 4:33

SAVIOUR - Jesus is Lord and Saviour. He saved His people by dying to redeem them, by giving the Holy Spirit to renew them by His power, by enabling them to overcome their spiritual enemies, by sustaining them in tribulation and in death, and by raising them up at the last day. *And she shall bring forth a son, and thou shalt call his name Jesus: for he shall save his people from their sins. Also, For unto you is born this day in the city of David a **Saviour**, which is Christ the Lord. And, Thou shalt also suck the milk of the Gentiles, and shalt suck the breast of kings: and thou shalt know that I the Lord am thy **Saviour** and thy Redeemer, the mighty One of Jacob.* Matthew 1:21; Luke 2:11; Isaiah 60:16

TRUE VINE - Jesus is the true vine who supplies to the branches (believer). Our life is in Christ, and He furnishes all we need in this lifetime and our new eternal life. *I am the **true vine**, and my Father is the husbandman.* John 15:1

WAY, TRUTH, LIFE - Jesus is our mediator and only pathway to the Father. There is no other means of securing a relationship with God and obtaining eternal life with the Father and His Son, but by Christ. *Jesus saith unto him, I am **the way, the truth, and the life**: no man cometh unto the Father, but by me.* John 14:6

Blood of Christ

C hrist shed blood from seven areas of His body to release man from the sins placed by the first Adam. These wounds represent a purpose in the Kingdom that man may be redeemed for reconciliation with the Father.

For Christ also hath once suffered for sins, the just for the unjust, that he might bring us to God, being put to death in the flesh, but quickened by the Spirit.
1 Peter 3:18

1) GARDEN OF GETHSEMANE

In the Garden of Gethsemane on the night of the Last Supper before He was taken, Christ sweats blood through His pores when blood vessels break beneath the skin. Alone, He prayed in agony to the Father knowing what was to occur.

And being in an agony he prayed more earnestly: and his sweat was as it were great drops of blood falling down to the ground. Luke 22:44

2) WHIPPING POST

Jesus was scourged an unaccountable number at the whipping post for all manner of healing. Infirmities, whether physical or emotional, have been dealt with along with our sins and transgressions.

Who his own self bare our sins in his own body on the tree, that we, being dead to sins, should live unto righteousness: by whose stripes ye were healed. 1 Peter 2:24

3) CROWN OF THORNS

He was taken to the chief priests and elders, and a crown of thorns was made and place on His head to make a mockery of Jesus.

And when they had platted a crown of thorns, they put it upon his head, and a reed in his right hand: and they bowed the knee before him, and mocked him, saying, Hail, King of the Jews! Matthew 27:29

4) NAILS IN THE HANDS

The palm of His hands bled from the nails that pierced His skin.

For dogs have compassed me: the assembly of the wicked have enclosed me: they pierced my hands and my feet. Psalm 22:16

5) NAILS IN THE FEET

Blood dripped from His feet as they were nailed to the cross.

Behold my hands and my feet, that it is I myself: handle me, and see; for a spirit hath not flesh and bones, as ye see me have. And when he had thus spoken, he showed them his hands and his feet. Luke 24:39-40 (after Christ's resurrection)

6) SPEAR IN THE SIDE

Jesus was pierced in the side by a soldier's spear after He died.

But one of the soldiers with a spear pierced his side, and forthwith came there out blood and water. John 19:34

7) INTERNAL BLEEDING AND BRUISING

Blood bruises on the outside of His skin reflective of internal bleeding.

I have glorified thee on the earth: I have finished the work which thou gavest me to do. John 17:4

And when Jesus had cried with a loud voice, he said, Father, into thy hands I commend my spirit: and having said thus, he gave up the ghost. Luke 23:46

Glory to Almighty God, Most High!

Seven Final Words of Jesus on the Cross

As Jesus hung on the Cross at Calvary, He spoke seven final statements before succumbing to His death. Notice seven phrases, the holy number of God.

THE FIRST WORD

Then said Jesus, **Father, forgive them; for they know not what they do.** Luke 23:34

THE SECOND WORD

Jesus speaks to the man on the cross beside him. *And he said to Jesus, Lord, remember me when thou comest into thy kingdom. And Jesus said unto him,* **Verily, I say to unto thee, to day shalt thou be with me in paradise.** Luke 23:42-43

THE THIRD WORD

When Jesus therefore saw his mother, and the disciple standing by, whom he loved, he saith unto his mother, **Woman, behold thy son!** *Then saith he to the disciple,* **Behold thy mother!** *And from that hour that disciple took her unto his home.* John 19:26-27

THE FOURTH WORD

And about the ninth hour, Jesus cried with a loud voice, saying, **Eli, Eli, lama sabachthani?** *That is to say,* **My God, my God, why have you forsaken me?** Matthew 27:46; Mark 15:34

THE FIFTH WORD

Jesus cried out in a loud voice, **Father, into your hands I commend my spirit.** Luke 23:46

THE SIXTH WORD

After this, Jesus knowing that all things were now accomplished, that the scripture might be fulfilled, saith, **I thirst.** John 19:28

THE SEVENTH WORD

Now there was set a vessel full of vinegar: and they filled a sponge with vinegar, and put it upon hyssop, and put it to his mouth. When Jesus therefore received the vinegar, he said, **It is finished**: *and he bowed his head, and gave up the ghost.* John 19:29-30

God's Seven Covenants

Between the first and last covenants, Adam to Christ, there are five additional covenants. God's creation is seven days and He established seven covenants that correlate with these days. Each covenant (contract) has a symbol (representation) and a seal (confirmation). As we know, seven days equates to seven thousand years. The first four covenants are from the Old Testament (four thousand years) and the last two covenants are of the New Testament (two thousand years). We are living in the last days of the sixth day of creation, or the six thousand years to be followed by the final one thousand year reign of Christ in the Kingdom of Peace.

Covenants of God

1) **ADAM**

> Symbol - Ground of the Earth
> Seal - The skin of the animals for a covering for
>   Adam and Eve
> Note: Man was made from the dust of the earth,
>   and the flesh will return to dust of the earth.

2) **NOAH**

Symbol - Rainbow
Seal - Noah sacrifices one of every clean animal
Note: God promises to not judge man again with
a flood of water.

3) **ABRAHAM**

Symbol - Stars
Seal - Circumcise of the foreskin of males;
Changing Abram's name to Abraham
Note: God tells Abraham for the number of stars
in the sky, so will he be the father of as
many children.

4) **MOSES**

Symbol - Tablets of Stone (Ten Commandments)
Seal - Broken by Moses (rewritten)
Note: God met with the Israelites at Mount Sinai
and gave the people statutes, ordinances,
judgments, and laws. God imposed a
covenant administered by Moses.

5) **DAVID**

Symbol - House of David (Israel)
Seal - The sacrifices on the alter in the temple
(Jerusalem)

Note: King David's son, Solomon, (appointed by
   God) built a temple to honor God. The
   temple is called Jerusalem, and the
   Israelites brought their sacrifices to this
   alter to worship God.

6) **MESSIAH**

Symbol - Christ
Seal - Cup of wine and bread at the Last Supper,
   representative of the body and blood of
   Jesus
Note: Christ spoke to His disciples at the Last
   Supper and made a covenant using
   wine and bread as representation of
   His body broken for man. The covenant
   was He would send the Holy Spirit,
   empowering them (and generations thereafter) with wisdom to continue teaching His
   gospel.

7) **PEACE**

Symbol - Christ
Seal - The word Shalom (peace) split into two
   words in the Scriptures
Note: Christ returns for the saints and we live with
   Him our King, in the Kingdom of Peace for
   one-thousand years before entering our
   final home, the New Jerusalem.

Spirit Gifts

Now concerning spiritual gifts brethren,
I would not have you ignorant.
1 Corinthians 12:1

There are gifts from the holy trinity of God, the Father; Christ, the Son; and the Holy Ghost. The gifts of God are all encompassing and divided among Christ and the Holy Spirit. God's gifts are administrative in the function of His Kingdom. Christ's gifts are for the continuation of His ministry. Though He is no longer a physical presence on the Earth, Christ lives within each believer, and we are to be disciples of His ministry. The gifts of the Holy Spirit are for interpretation of God's Word, so we may learn of the Kingdom, have a relationship with the Father, and do His will. With the ability to receive heavenly gifts and power through the Holy Spirit, we may live a spirit-filled life for the glory of God's Kingdom.

Now there are diversities of gifts, but the same Spirit. And there are differences of administrations, but the same Lord. And there are diversities of operations, but it is the same God which worketh all in all. 1 Corinthians 12:4-6

Gifts of God - Administration

Apostle, Prophets, Teachers, Miracles, Healings, Helps, Governments, and Diversities of Tongues

Now ye are the body of Christ, and members in particular. And God hath set some in the church, first apostles, secondarily prophets, thirdly teachers, after that miracles, then gifts of healings, helps, governments, diversities of tongues. Are all apostles? Are all prophets? are all teachers? are all workers of miracles? Have all the gifts of healing? do all speak with tongues? do all interpret? But covet earnestly the best gifts: and yet show I unto you a more excellent way. 1 Corinthians 12:17-31

God's gifts are established within His Kingdom and dispensed through the trinity of Christ and the Holy Ghost according to His purpose for man.

Gifts of Christ - Ministry

Apostles, Prophets, Evangelists, Pastors, and Teachers

Now that he ascended, what is it but that he also descended first into the lower parts of the earth? He that descended is the same also that ascended up far above all heavens, that he might fill all things. And he gave

some, <u>apostles</u>; and some, <u>prophets</u>; and some, <u>evangelists</u>; and some, <u>pastors</u> and <u>teachers</u>; For the perfecting of the saints, for the work of the ministry, for the edifying of the body of Christ. Ephesians 4:9-12

Christ's gifts are for the ministry of the Kingdom of Heaven. We have many individuals professing the gospel of Christ, but it should be noted that Jesus chooses who will be the true apostles of His ministry, for He knows their heart is pure with obedience to receiving and edifying His Word. Though, it should be stated that each faithful believer in truth to His Word and directed by the Spirit of Truth is a disciple of the gospel of Christ.

Gifts of the Holy Spirit - Power

Wisdom, Knowledge, Faith, Healing, Miracles, Prophecy, Discerning of Spirits, Speaking in Tongues, Inter-pretation of Tongues

But the manifestation of the Spirit is given to every man to profit withal. For to one is given by the Spirit the word of <u>wisdom</u>; to another the word of <u>knowledge</u> by the same Spirit; To another <u>faith</u> by the same Spirit; to another the gifts of <u>healing</u> by the same Spirit; To another the working of <u>miracles</u>; to another <u>prophecy</u>; to another <u>discerning of spirits</u>; to another <u>divers kinds of tongues</u>; to another the <u>interpretation of tongues</u>: But all these worth that one and the selfsame Spirit, dividing to every man severally as he will. 1 Corinthians 12:7-11

Notice the Holy Spirit gives the most gifts. In the Holy Spirit, God has provided all that we will need in this lifetime. The Holy Spirit gives us our education in God's Word and teaches the principles of the Kingdom. He grants us the ability to interpret the truth from inaccurate teachings, helps in the appropriation of our faith that we may receive the Father's gifts and supernatural power, and that we edify God in the most intimate manner by speaking in a heavenly, spiritual language.

We can be given more than one gift, but we should understand that with the gifts also is the Holy Spirit providing the utterance of when to apply them. We are not presented a gift and left on our own merit because in reality we wouldn't use it properly. There would be the natural inclination to apply our personal perception and preference. Spiritual gifts are pure and holy requiring guidance to make them effectual. It is supernatural power, and we are the vessels it flows through.

Having then gifts differing according to the grace that is given to us, whether prophecy, let us prophesy according to the proportion of faith; Or ministry, let us wait on our ministering: or he that teacheth, on teaching; Or he that exhorteth,on exhortation: he that giveth, let him do it with simplicity; he that ruleth, with diligence; he that showeth mercy, with cheerfulness. Romans 12:6-8

It is noteworthy that the gifts are administered according to grace, for we live by the grace given as a gift in Jesus Christ.

Afflictions Upon Man

But let none of you suffer as a murderer, or
as a thief, or as an evildoer, or as a busybody
in other men's matters.
1 Peter 4:15

Bless them which persecute you: bless, and
curse not.
Romans 12:14

The mere definition of affliction denotes a matter of distress, misery, or grief. A symbolic word more commonly misunderstood is the word, curses. Man causes many forms of afflictions upon himself, loved ones, friends, and strangers; individually, or as a society. The world events attest to this destruction. The cultural atmosphere has digressed into an ungodly state, and we are constantly under attack on a personal level as well as a national one. Whether we call it an affliction or a curse, someone has to initiate and inflict it.

There is a cause and effect ratio to everything in life, for it is an aspect of the balancing system. Curses have a negative affect and impact our lives, and we should be armored in God's Word to counter the attack.

Finally, my brethren, be strong in the Lord, and in the

power of his might. Put on the whole armor of God, that ye may be able to stand against the wiles of the devil. For we wrestle not against flesh and blood, but against principalities, against powers, against the rulers of the darkness of this world, against spiritual wickedness in high places. Wherefore take unto you the whole armor of God that ye may be able to withstand in the evil day, and having done all, to stand. Ephesians 6:10-13

Though God is telling us how to be prepared for spiritual warfare, His instructions also apply in the natural, or physical world. God gives us the arsenal to use in any battlefield. An invaluable strategy of being prepared is understanding your opponent.

These attacks come in the spoken word and can lay a heavy assault on the recipient. We have an innate ability to bring forth afflictions by not guarding our tongue. It is human nature to be influenced by the words told to us, over us, or about us. Often we accept derogatory comments as the truth, because they are spoken by people we know and care about which we believe warrants their comments. Unless we are polished with knowledge and understand how curses wreak havoc in our life, they go unchecked. The statements are never countered and nullified, destroying the curse before it takes root.

Let no corrupt communication proceed out of your mouth, but that which is good to the use of edifying, that it may minister grace unto the hearers. Ephesians 4:29

When we think of a curse, the first thought may be the use of profanity, harsh verbiage, or something far more demonic. There is the individual who belts out comments whether slated in humor, or a deliberate act, to purposefully cause emotional injury to the recipient. This can be the most dangerous because often the person has grown accustomed to the assault and declines to retaliate, thus, breaking the curse. They become immune to the offense, especially if it occurs often, but the damage remains.

In reality, it sticks with them and does emotional, psychological, and eventually physiological harm. This is tampering with the spirit and soul of the person, a definite sin. Just because someone is unprepared to fight back, or block the curse, it is spiritually unlawful to place harm on another whether orally, or physically.

We should not let our guard down in warfare. What appears on the surface to be a battle among ourselves, never underestimate that the underlying current is of a spiritual nature. If you believe a curse has a stronghold on your life, or those you love, rebuke the words spoken. Curses do affect our lives whether we believe it, or not.

But I say unto you, Love your enemies, bless them that curse you do good to them that hate you, and pray for them which despitefully use you, and persecute you. Matthew 5:44

MAN - When a person speaks unfavorably, or negatively over someone whom they have a responsibility or authoritative jurisdiction, the individual can place a curse when using negative comments. For example, a parent to a child, or child to an elderly parent, employer to an employee, and so forth. A parent can easily bring a curse upon their children with the very words they speak over, to, and about them with such comments as, *He's always sick.* or *She isn't my brightest child.* Confrontations with family, friends, and colleagues can release accusations whereby the words spoken may have negative connotation, or implications. There is power, be it for good or harm, in the spoken language.

For God commanded, saying, Honour thy father and mother: and, He that curseth father or mother, let him die the death. Matthew 15:4

SELF-INFLICTED - What are we saying about ourselves? If we are speaking negatively about our body, or state of being, then we are placing a curse on our life. For example, *I'm just not smart enough.* or *I guess I was meant to be a fat person, I can't seem to lose the weight.* Such statements hold us in bondage to the very words we speak which can be a reason for not succeeding in our endeavors. Making derogatory comments opposes the Kingdom. As a child of the Father, our body is a temple. We belong to God and in speaking ill-favorably of ourselves, it is an assault to Him.

What? know ye not that your body is the temple of the Holy Ghost which is in you, which ye have of God, and ye are not your own? 1 Corinthians 6:19

SOWING AND REAPING - What we do is what we get, figuratively and literally. Doing bad things reaps hardship in our future, and equally so, doing good deeds according to God's Word will supply benefits and blessings hundredfold. What we do in this lifetime does make a difference now and forever.

And he that reapeth receiveth wages, and gathereth fruit unto life eternal: that both he that soweth and he that reapeth may rejoice together. John 4:36

PROPHETS - Refrain from speaking unkindly of the individuals who are in truth to the Spirit of Truth because in doing so we are speaking against the trinity of God: the Father, the Son, and the Holy Ghost. It becomes blasphemy against the Kingdom of Heaven and is against Christ's chosen people for His ministry.

He suffered no man to do them wrong: yea, he reproved kings for their sakes, Saying;Touch not mine anointed, and do my prophets no harm. Psalm 105:14-15

THE ACCUSED - Being around someone who is cursed can bring that curse upon ourselves; however, let's qualify this statement. This is not referring to a curse rubbing off on us if we get to close to someone who is afflicted, but rather if we are not strong in our knowledge of Kingdom principles and hold firm to deflect the enemy, we can have their curse applied to us and not be aware of what is transpiring. This is easily performed in our communications when we accept derogatory words spoken about someone, and jump right in and start believing and conversing over the matter and take on the same mindset, spreading the negative.

Follow peace with all men, and holiness, without which no man shall see the Lord: Looking diligently lest any man fail of the grace of God; lest any root of bitterness springing up troubled you,and thereby many be defiled.

Hebrews 12:14-15

INHERITANCE - Curses that carry down through generations in a family and are unbeknown to the members. We curse ourselves and others by making such statements as, *My grandmother had it, my mother has it, and I guess I was next in line to get it.* Another generational curse is spreading negativity with such words as, *He isn't going to amount to anything.* Statements such as these are destroying families.

To open their eyes, and to turn them from darkness to light, and from the power of Satan unto God, that they may receive forgiveness of sins, and inheritance among them which are sanctified by the faith that is in me. Acts 26:18

UNFORGIVING - When we choose to live in bitterness without forgiveness towards someone, it makes us an accuser. It is a command of God that we forgive those who trespass against us, for whatever the reason. If we cannot forgive others, our Father will not forgive us. Forgiveness is mandatory in the Kingdom of Heaven.

Then came Peter to him, and said, Lord, how oft shall my brother sin against me, and I forgive him? till seven times? Jesus saith unto him, I say not unto thee, until seven times: but, until seventy times seven. Matthew 18:21-22

THE LAW - When the laws of the Kingdom are broken, it makes us vulnerable for Satan to gain entrance into our life. Satan's only inroad is when we are unfaithful to God's Word. We must repent and get back into the grace of God.

For I delight in the law of God after the inward man. Romans 7:22

And knowest his will, and approvest the things that are more excellent, being instructed out of the law. Romans 2:18

I thank God through Jesus Christ our Lord. So then with the mind I myself serve the law of God; but with the flesh the law of sin. Romans 7:25

For the law of the Spirit of life in Christ Jesus hath made me free from the law of sin and death. Romans 8:2

DEMONIC - As faithful children of God under the hedge of protection within the Kingdom, Satan cannot reach us. It is through our thoughts that he deceives, so we must guard our mind; rebuke and repent anything that is not in truth to the Father's Word. The mind is the only means by which we can falter and come under attack of the enemy. If we do, Satan uses his deceitful wiles against us for the sole purpose of destruction, for the finality of death.

The thief cometh not, but for to steal, and to kill, and to destroy: I am come that they might have life, and that they might have it more abundantly. John 10:10

And there shall be no more curse: but the throne of God and of the Lamb shall be in it; and his servants shall serve him. Revelation 22:3

Identification of Personal Blocks

There are many things that can block the power of God from entering into our life. It only takes one to obstruct the pathway. We should take a serious look at each of the following and determine if any apply as the reason for not receiving a healing.

1) Unforgiving

*For if ye **forgive** men their trespasses, your heavenly Father will also **forgive** you: But if ye **forgive** not men their trespasses, neither will your Father **forgive** your trespasses.* Mark 6:14-15

Holding grudges blocks love. If we do not forgive those who have done injustices towards us, how then can we expect God to forgive us. God tells us in His Word and is very explicit in His command: *Beloved, let us love one another: for love is of God; and every one that loveth is born of God, and knoweth God.* 1 John 4:7 It cannot be explained any more succinctly than this. God requires that we have brotherly love for each other and when we face objection, then we forgive the person their wrongdoing and walk away. *Verily I say unto you, Inasmuch as ye have done it unto one of the least of these my brethren, ye have done it unto me.* Matthew 25:40

Pray for forgiveness of anything you are harboring in your heart against another, so that you release any bondage that has entrapped you within.

2) Strife

*Hatred stirreth up **strifes**: but love covereth all sins.* Proverbs 10:12

Strife is a complex matter. It encompasses so many things in our life from how we feel about ourselves, to our relationships with our loved ones, to how we interact with others. It can be born of an emotional or spiritual nature and when not recognized, can be very destructive in hearing from God and receiving healing power. *A wrathful man stirreth up strife: but he that is slow to anger appeaseth strife.* Proverbs 15:18 Anger, contention, upheaval, meddling, and so forth bring strife and discontent among family and friends which causes disharmony. *It is an honor for a man to cease from strife: but every fool will be meddling.* Proverbs 20:3

3) Curses

*Bless them which persecute you: bless, and **curse** not.* Romans 12:14

By the very words we speak, we can curse ourselves and others. Negative words whether spoken in humor or seriousness, places bondage on the person spoken to or about. God instructs us to guard our tongue for there is power in our words, just as there is power in

God's Word. Curses are real and do affect our life and our health. Man causes many forms of afflictions upon himself, loved ones, friends, and strangers; individually, or as a society. *But I say unto you, Love your enemies, bless them that curse you, do good to them that hate you, and pray for them which despitefully use you, and persecute you.* Matthew 5:44 Be armored in God's Word and pray that any curses, known or not, be removed from your life and the lives of your loved ones. *Pleasant words are as an honeycomb, sweet to the soul, and health to the bones.* Proverbs 16:24 It is only a prayer away to receive freedom from a curse.

4) Fear

*For God hath not given us the spirit of **fear**, but of power, and of love, and of a sound mind.* 1 Timothy 1:7

If we are in fear then we cannot be in faith, for fear voids faith. Fear is a negative emotion and is not of God. Fear is an emotional response that renders uncertainty and confusion. *For ye have not received the spirit of bondage again to fear; but ye have received the Spirit of adoption, whereby we cry, Abba, Father.* Romans 8:15 Fear draws us away from God's promises and holds us captive to the emotion which affects our decisions. When fear arises, it should be immediately replaced with faith. We must hold strong and allow our faith to command over fear, and trust in the Father's Word.

Therefore being justified by faith we have peace with God through our Lord Jesus Christ: By whom also we have access by faith into this grace wherein we stand, and rejoice in hope of the glory of God. Romans 5:1-2

5) Pride

For all that is in the world, the lust of the flesh, and the lust of the eyes, and the **pride** *of life, is not of the Father, but is of the world.* 1 John 2:16

Pride is an interesting subject because its often misconstrued as confidence. What we consider to be confidence in ourselves can in actuality be pride, so how do we distinguish the difference? *The wicked, through the pride of his countenance, will not seek after God: God is not in all his thoughts.* Psalm 10:4 God doesn't accept pridefulness. Typically, a prideful person will seldom change their mind, nor accept they could be incorrect, and believe they know best. However, a confident individual will ponder and accept evaluation and make the necessary changes accordingly without losing their confidence. *A man's pride shall bring him low; but honor shall uphold the humble in spirit.* Proverbs 29:23 Often, we don't see this element within ourselves, but it's a major stumbling block to receiving from God.

6) Guilt

Deliver me from blood **guiltiness***, O God of my salvation: and my tongue shall sing aloud of thy righteousness.* Psalm 51:14

We can all find reason to feel guilty about something we have said or done in our lifetime; how-ever, it is what we do with guilt that determines if we remain in bondage to our thoughts and feelings. When guilty of a word or act, asking forgiveness and letting go is the healthy thing to do. *Accuse not a servant unto his master, lest he curse thee, and though be found guilty.* Proverbs 30:10 Don't hold onto guilt because it will surely strip you from living in righteousness as you are meant to do in Christ.

7) Shame

O my god, I trust in thee: let me not be **ashamed**, *let not mine enemies triumph over me.* Psalm 25:2

Shame comes from an outside source usually because of something someone has said or done that destroys our self-worth, self-esteem, and self-confidence making us feel unworthy. There can also be occasions when we bring shame upon ourselves by our own actions. This is a dangerous mindset because its roots are destructive and emotionally paralyzing. *For the scripture saith, Whosoever believeth on him shall not be ashamed.* Roman 10:11 In Christ, we are cleansed and made righteous by His blood whereby there is no shame. As with sin, shame is washed away by the blood of Jesus. *According to my earnest expectation and my hope, that in nothing I shall be ashamed, but that with all boldness, as always, so now also Christ shall be mag-nified in my body, whether it be by life, or by my death.* Philippians 1:20 If there is shame within your soul, remember you are free from sin and shame. You are always worthy in the eyes of the Lord.

8) Grief

*Surely he hath borne our **griefs**, and carried our sorrows: yet we did esteem him stricken, smitten of God, and afflicted.* Isaiah 53:4

Everyone experiences grief and perhaps the most commonly know is the loss of a loved one; grief due to death is difficult. There is also grief from the termination of a relationship or friendship, or from accidents that leave someone physically challenged. There are many things that can cause grief but it's not a state of mind to remain in. Grief can quickly take our happiness, peace, and joy away leaving us feeling hopeless and helpless. *But if any have caused grief, he hath not grieved me, but in part: that I may not overcharge you all. Sufficient to such a man is this punishment, which was inflicted of many. So that contrariwise ye ought rather to forgive him, and comfort him, lest perhaps such a one should be swallowed up with overmuch sorrow. Wherefore I beseech you that ye would confirm your love toward him.* 2 Corinthians 2:5-8 Don't allow grief to consume you, break free that your life may be of joy and peace in Christ.

9) Idolatry

*Wherefore, my dearly beloved, flee from **idolatry**.* 1 Corinthians 10:14

Idolatry is a clever and dangerous element when our attention is focused on persons or things making them important in our lives. It is critical to be very astute in this area and not allow possessions or interests to predominate our thoughts and desires. *Mortify therefore your members which are upon the earth; fornication, uncleanness, inordinate affection, evil concupiscence, and covetousness, which is idolatry.* Colossians 3:5 Fascinations can easily turn into obsessions and take us in a direction whereby we are more mindful of our desires rather than astute to God. *Now the works of the flesh are manifest, which are these; Adultery, fornication, uncleanness, lasciviousness, idolatry, witchcraft, hatred, emulations, wrath, strife, seditions, heresies, envying, murders, drunkenness, revelings, and such like: of the which I tell you before, and I have also told you in time past, that they which do such things shall not inherit the kingdom of God.* Galatians 5:19-21

10) Hopelessness

*For we are saved by **hope**: but **hope** that is seen is not **hope**: for what man seeth, why doth he yet **hope** for? But if we **hope** for that we see not, then do we with patience wait for it.* Romans 8:24-25

Our foundation of faith is based on hope. Hope brings the unseen, the things of God, into existence through our continual faith as we pray and stand in hope for what we seek will manifest into our lives. It is hope we cleave to as we hold firm in faith and patiently await the heavenly outcome. *Hope deferred makes the heart sick: but when the desire cometh, it is a tree of life.* Proverbs 13:12 Hope is a critical element in faith defined as the substance of having faith. *The hope of the righteous shall be gladness: but the expectation of the wicked shall perish.* Proverbs 10:28 Never give up hope in God's ability to supply for your needs. Remember, hope is just as important as faith because it is a component of faith. *Therefore did my heart rejoice, and my tongue was glad; moreover also my flesh shall rest in hope.* Acts 2:26 Cleave to hope in faith and you shall receive the blessings our heavenly Father has promised.

11) Thanklessness

*Enter into his gates with **thanksgiving**, and into his courts with praise: be **thankful** unto him, and bless his name.* Colossians 3:15

In all of life, give praise, honor, glory, and thanksgiving to the Lord for His mercy and grace, and His blessings and promises, for they are bountiful. *Being enriched in every thing to all bountifulness, which causeth through us thanksgiving to God.* 2 Corinthians 9:11 We often forget to thank our heavenly Father for all the wonderful things He has done through His Son. We must not become ungrateful; therefore, if we are limited in our thanksgiving we can easily slip into thoughtlessness. *For the administration of this service not only supplieth the want of the saints, but is abundant also by many thanksgivings unto God.* 2 Corinthians 9:11-12 We thank each other upon receiving gifts, much more should we remember to thank God for His mighty gifts.

12) Lack of Patience

*And besides this, giving all diligence, add to your faith virtue; and to virtue knowledge; And to knowledge temperance; and to temperance **patience**; and to **patience** godliness; And to godliness brotherly kindness; and to brotherly kindness charity. 2 Peter 1:5-7*

Patience is truly a virtue and commendable before the Lord. In our deliverance from troubled times, a rough passage in our daily life, we are to have patience as God's resolution manifest. During this hardship, our patience is shown in our unrelenting and steadfast faith. Patience is a direct reflection of our maintaining faith in our moment of crisis and holding to His Word.

According as his divine power hath given unto us all things that pertain unto life and godliness, through the knowledge of him that hath called us to glory and virtue. 2 Peter 1:3

Living in a fallen world, an imperfect environment, is going to breed mishaps and offensive situations; however, in our faith we have hope, and with hope, we gain patience, and through patience we acquire virtue. All work towards the attaining of the supernatural power of the Holy Spirit by the authority given in Christ.

My brethren, count it all joy when ye fall into divers temptations; Knowing this, that the trying of your faith worketh patience. But let patience have her perfect work that ye may be perfect and entire, wanting nothing. James 1:2-4

13) Lack of Faith

*Therefore being justified by faith we have peace with God through our Lord Jesus Christ: By whom also we have access by **faith** into this grace wherein we stand, and rejoice in hope of the glory of God.* Romans 5:1-5

Without faith we are lost to anything of the Kingdom of Heaven. All treasures of blessings, gifts, and promises are void to our life when we do not have faith. Jesus said only a small amount of true faith will open the Kingdom doors to receive. However, along with faith, we stay in hope of the anticipation of the answers to our prayers. We wait for the unseen to become the seen, the supernatural power from heaven to be witnessed in the natural.

For I say, through the grace given unto me, to every man that is among you, not to think of himself more highly than he ought to think; but to think soberly, according as God hath dealt to every man the measure of faith. Romans 12:3

Faith is our stronghold to all answered prayers, the key to the Kingdom of Heaven.

14) Lack of Love

*And we have known and believed in the **love** that God hath for us. God is **love**; and he that dwelleth in **love** dwelleth in God, and God in him.* 1 John 4:16

Love is a word that is spoken frequently but often without meaning. It easily becomes second nature to apply the word love in our signature statements, but do we truly mean it when we say it? Love begins with loving God and understanding the very nature of His love. From His agape love, we learn to love ourselves and accept ourselves worthy to be loved, so that we may be equipped to love another. Love surpasses all things, and makes all things complete as God teaches us in His perfect love for His children.

And thou shalt love the Lord thy God with all thy heart, and with all thy soul, and with all thy mind, and with all thy strength: this is the first commandment. And the second is like, namely this, Thou shalt love thy neighbor as thyself. There is none other commandment greater than these. Mark 12:30-31

Love is the beginning and the end to all things of God; and likewise, is the beginning to our faith, our hope, our patience, our forgiveness, and so forth. It all begins with love. We must have a heart of love to conquer hatred, anger, disillusionment, disappointment, discouragement, and the list goes on.

15) Double-minded

*A **double minded** man is unstable in all his ways.* James 1:8

Having two sets of standards to suit the occasion is not worthy of any attention and does not make for accountability in our relationship with our heavenly Father, nor with those we are close with. It makes us unreliable and untrustworthy. *Draw nigh to God, and he will draw nigh to you. Cleanse your hands, ye sinners; and purify your hearts, ye double minded.* James 4:8 Hold to one standard, one belief, one trusting nature in all matters, and be sure that it is in the Lord.

16) Ignorance

*For they being **ignorant** of God's righteousness, and going about to establish their own righteousness, have not submitted themselves unto the righteousness of God.* Romans 10:3

As a child of the Father, ignorance of His Word will never be an acceptable excuse. Becoming born-again to the spiritual being we are in Christ, we then accept our journey into learning how to live our new spirit life as we remain in the natural. We cannot claim, *I didn't know,* and have expectations of God. Maybe our children can use that excuse with us from time to time when they haven't been obedient, but it doesn't work that way as children of God.

But if any man be ignorant, let him be ignorant. 1 Corinthians 14:38

If your choice is to not know God's Word, then remain without knowledge, but don't expect Kingdom privileges.

17) Judgmental

***Judge** not, that ye be not **judged**. For with what **judgment** ye **judge**, ye shall be **judged** and with what*

measure ye mete, it shall be measured to you again.
Matthew 7:2

God is very explicit in His Word. If we choose to judge others based on our opinion, then what we hold them in unfavorableness will be placed on us, and God will measure equal judgment onto us. We all have opinions, and it is easy to find fault with another simply by reason of not agreeing, but it is a dangerous mindset to speak accusations of disapproval in judgment.

Judge not, and ye shall not be judged condemn not, and ye shall not be condemned: forgive, and ye shall be forgiven. Give, and it shall be given unto you; good measure, pressed down, and shaken together, and running over, shall men give into your bosom. For with the same measure that ye mete withal it shall be measured to you again. Luke 6:37-38

Let a man so account of us, as of the ministers of Christ, and stewards of the mysteries of God. Moreover it is required in stewards, that a man be found faithful. But with me it is a very small thing that I should be judged of you, or of man's judgment: yea, I judge not mine own self. For I know nothing by myself; yet am I not hereby justified: but he that judge me is the Lord. 1 Corinthians 4:1-4

God is the only One who passes judgment. We will all stand before Christ on the Judgement Day and be held accountable for our earthen behavior. Because of our carnal tendencies, we often slip in this arena; however, when we find ourselves voicing our opinion in judgement of another, we should take notice and withdraw our statement of accusation.

For what have I to do to judge them also that are without? Do not ye judge them that are within? But them that are without God judgeth. Therefore put away from among yourselves that wicked person. 1 Corinthians 5:12-13 God calls us wicked who judges another. In John 8:15-16, *Ye judge after the flesh, I judge no man. And yet if I judge, my judgment is true: for I am not alone, but I and the Father that sent me.* There is only One who may pass judgment. There is a difference between disapproval and placing judgment on another person.

18) Unbelief

And he did not many mighty works there because of there unbelief. Matthew 13:58

There I say unto you, What things soever ye desire, when ye pray, believe that ye receive them, and ye shall have them. Mark 11:24

Without belief, we are in unbelief. It begins with believing in the Lord and relying on His Word; being faithful, obedient, and trusting in hope for the manifestation of His blessings, and knowing it will be forthcoming. We may think ourselves faithful, but doubt can be just as prevalent as our belief, and it can wash away our belief in an instant. Jesus said unto him: *if thou canst believe, all things are possible to him that believeth. And straightway the father of the child cried out, and said with tears, Lord, I believe; help thou mine unbelief.* Mark 9:23-24 When we doubt to seeing the supernatural power of God exemplified in the natural, we have voided our prayer of faith. This is the major reason many do not receive from God. Though they believe their faith to be strong, there can be question-able doubt, unbelief.

Just as we learn in the Bible of the miracles and healing by God as reflected in the Old Testament and by Jesus in the New Testament, they are still prevalent today in our lifetime. However, as God and His Son performed the miracles and healing in past gen-erations, we are responsible through faith and belief to acquire them in our generation. Know how to receive the supernatural power in the Kingdom to heal yourself and others. Christ has given to each faithful believer His authority within the Kingdom of Heaven, and through the Holy Spirit, to receive that which we ask. Do not allow unbelief to block God's supernatural power from flowing continuously in your life.

Unbelief prevents us from having a relationship with our heavenly Father. Of all the obstacles that can block our communication and commitment to God, unbelief trumps all others.

Prayer of Protection

Psalm 91

He that dwelleth in the secret place of the most High shall abide under the shadow of the Almighty. I will say of the Lord, He is my refuge and my fortress: my God; in him will I trust. Surely he shall deliver thee from the snare of the fowler, and from the noisome pestilence. He shall cover thee with his feathers, and under his wings shalt thou trust: his truth shall be thy shield and buckler. Thou shalt not be afraid for the terror by night; nor for the arrow that flieth by day; Nor for the pestilence that walketh in darkness; nor for the destruction that wasteth at noonday. A thousand shall fall at thy side, and ten thousand at thy right hand; but it shall not come nigh thee. Only with thine eyes shalt thou behold and see the reward of the wicked. Because thou hast made the Lord, which is my refuge, even the most High, thy habitation; There shall no evil befall thee, neither shall any plague come nigh thy dwelling. For he shall give his angels charge over thee, to keep thee in all thy ways. They shall bear thee up in their hands, lest thou dash thy foot against a stone. Thou shalt tread upon the lion and adder: the young lion and the dragon shalt thou trample under feet. Because he hath set his love upon me, therefore will I deliver him: I will set him on high, be-cause he hath known my name. He shall call upon me, and I will answer him: I will be with him in trouble; I will deliver him, and honour him. With long life will I satisfy him, and shew him my salvation.

Armor of God

Ephesians 6:10-18

Finally, my brethren, be strong in the Lord, and in the power of his might. Put on the whole armour of God, that ye may be able to stand against the wiles of the devil. For we wrestle not against flesh and blood, but against principalities, against powers, against the rulers of the darkness of this world, against spiritual wickedness in high places. Wherefore take unto you the whole armour of God, that ye may be able to withstand in the evil day, and having done all, to stand. Stand therefore, having your loins girt about with truth, and having on the breastplate of righteousness; And your feet shod with the preparation of the gospel of peace; Above all, taking the shield of faith, wherewith ye shall be able to quench all the fiery darts of the wicked. And take the helmet of salvation, and the sword of the Spirit, which is the word of God: Praying always with all prayer and supplication in the Spirit, and watching thereunto with all perseverance and supplication for all saints.

Everlasting Love, God's Greatest Gift

EXCERPT

Everlasting Love, God's Greatest Gift reveals the love of the Father for His children. From the beginning of Creation, God fashioned the heavens and the earth for you with an enduring and *everlasting love*, never forgotten or forsaken. Mercy, grace, faith, blessings, promises, gifts, and supernatural power abound to the faithful children of the Almighty King. We are sons and daughters, heirs in Christ within the Kingdom of Heaven with the privilege to come before the throne of our Lord.

Everlasting Love, God's Greatest Gift presents an intimate journey into the trinity of God as the Father, the Son, and the Holy Ghost; the trinity of man created with a spirit, soul, and body; and the Kingdom of Heaven which functions with mercy, grace, and faith.

We obtain a life-altering makeover through the blood of Christ and given the gift of faith to unlock the mysteries of God's Kingdom that we may obtain His dunamis power to defeat fear, anxiety, depression, confusion, illness, disease, heartache, financial disparity, and addictions. God intends for His children to overcome and triumph in any adversity and be set free from whatever holds you captive as the result of living in a fallen world.

Take the key of faith, place it in the Kingdom lock, and turn to the truth in His Word to open a new beginning in your life today. Live as a rightful heir of the Almighty King of the Kingdom of Heaven, secure and sealed in the Father's *Everlasting Love*.

This book includes a study guide beneficial for individual or group participation. In addition, spirit topics are included with a comprehensive look at the nature, works, and position of the Son of God in the trinity of the Father, the Son, and the Holy Ghost.

About the Author

Patricia Marlett is dedicated to writing inspirational novels for both the adult and young reader genres. She pens plots that reflect real life events through drama, intrigue, suspense, humor, and love. A faith inspiring messages is subtly woven within the endearing themes of her stories lending to heartfelt expressions from laughter to tears and always with hope and joy.

Patricia also enjoys writing non-fiction books about our heavenly Father and His Son along with the gift of the Holy Spirit. Within these books, details the nature and love of God and the life of Christ.

Visit Patricia at her website, www.patriciamarlett.com, to learn of her passion for writing, view her books, and for contact information.

www.ingramcontent.com/pod-product-compliance
Lightning Source LLC
LaVergne TN
LVHW051635080426
835511LV00016B/2348